MW01154486

Mastering the Samurai Sword

Mastering the Samurai Sword

CARY NEMEROFF

A Full-Color, Step-by-Step Guide

DVD included!

TUTTLE PUBLISHING
Tokyo • Rutland, Vermont • Singapore

Published by Tuttle Publishing, an imprint of Periplus Editions (HK) Ltd., with editorial offices at 364 Innovation Drive, North Clarendon, Vermont 05759 U.S.A.

Library of Congress Cataloging-in-Publication Data
Nemeroff, Cary.
    Mastering the samurai sword : a full-color, step-by-step guide / Cary Nemeroff. — 1st ed.
        p. cm.
    ISBN 978-0-8048-3955-6 (pbk. : alk. paper)
    1. Swords—Japan. 2. Swordplay—Japan. I. Title.
    GV1150.2.N46 2008
    739.7'220952—dc22

                                        2008005618

ISBN-13: 978-0-8048-3955-6

Distributed by

North America, **Latin America & Europe**	**Japan**	**Asia Pacific**
Tuttle Publishing	Tuttle Publishing	Berkeley Books Pte. Ltd.
364 Innovation Drive	Yaekari Building, 3rd Floor	61 Tai Seng Avenue #02-12
North Clarendon, VT	5-4-12 Osaki	Singapore 534167
05759-9436 U.S.A.	Shinagawa-ku	Tel: (65) 6280-1330
Tel: 1 (802) 773-8930	Tokyo 141 0032	Fax: (65) 6280-6290
Fax: 1 (802) 773-6993	Tel: (81) 3 5437-0171	inquiries@periplus.com.sg
info@tuttlepublishing.com	Fax: (81) 3 5437-0755	www.periplus.com
www.tuttlepublishing.com	tuttle-sales@gol.com	

First edition
12 11 10 09   10 9 8 7 6 5 4 3 2

Printed in Hong Kong

TUTTLE PUBLISHING® is a registered trademark of Tuttle Publishing,
a division of Periplus Editions (HK) Ltd.

Contents

Foreword

I am sure that anyone who has an interest in the Japanese sword will appreciate this well-written and informative publication. Cary Nemeroff, Soke Shodai (first-generation head founder) of the Fukasa-Ryu martial arts system, is a highly skilled martial arts master who began training under me in 1977. He continues training on a regular basis, even though he is a founder of his own martial arts style.

Cary has always displayed an above-average ability to learn the martial arts. He excelled at everything he was taught, and many years later became my only student who earned *dan* ranking in nearly all of the martial arts that I teach and represent. This was quite an achievement on his part.

I introduced Cary to the sword many years ago, and it soon became his favorite weapon. He never missed a sword clinic and even had the honor of training in the early 1990s under Shihan Tomio Nakai of Japan (my last traditional Japanese sword *sensei*) during one of his training visits for Juko-Kai members.

Cary earned his *shihan* (master instructor) grading in my sokeship art of juko-ryu iai-jutsu/ken-jutsu, and, like all head founders, he developed his own sword *kata*. His forms are a reflection of what he feels his sword art should represent. It is my opinion that he has done a fine job in this respect.

—Rod Sacharnoski, Dai-Soke, Tenth Dan
President, Juko-Kai International
Ninth Dan Hanshi, Seidokan Karate, Kobudo and Toide

Preface

This book was originally designed as a manual for my own students. I hope it will become an invaluable resource for all students of kobu-jutsu, and certainly for those who are studying some form of iai-jutsu or ken-jutsu.

I will commence by taking the reader through what I term a brief history of Japan. Next, we will examine two major forms of the samurai fighting arts, which in Japanese are known as *kobu-jutsu*: the sword techniques of *iai-jutsu* and *ken-jutsu,* the drawing of the samurai sword and samurai sword fencing. These evolved by empirical means alone, as the samurai reflected upon their experiences in battle, and honed their technique by applying lessons learned using the battlefield as a laboratory.

Last, we will delve deeply into Fukasa-Ryu iai-jutsu and ken-jutsu, one modern *ryu* (style) of iai-jutsu and ken-jutsu that is deeply rooted in some of the oldest extant kobu-jutsu. When I use the word "modern" here, it is not meant in any way to imply that this is some sort of inauthentic, completely subjective ryu that evolved from a path different from other styles of kobu-jutsu that continue to exist today. In using the term "modern," I am attempting to accurately describe something that *is taught and learned today, contemplated today, and continues to evolve today.* Although it was named as a unique ryu in the modern era, modernity was not an intended component of this ryu, which respects and incorporates long-established kobu-jutsu techniques. This ryu's ideology, *saho* (formal etiquette), and *waza* (techniques) have all been conscientiously preserved in the original forms of the ryu that have come before it.

The Fukasa-Ryu way of iai-jutsu and ken-jutsu is the materialization and documentation of another samurai swordsman's retrospection upon his life, a retrospection that began with kobu-jutsu study during my childhood and remains a driving force manifesting itself in both my career and my personal life. In writing this book, I am not purporting to reinvent the wheel. I am, however, taking a painstaking look at a variety of well-made wheels and retrofitting them to a more modern car.

In recent years, the samurai sword has undergone one of the greatest transformations in its long history. While once used by a select class of warriors on the battlefield, it has now found its way into lives and classrooms around the world, as a tool for self-betterment, learning, and reflection.

Samurai sword training can have a positive effect on the body by calming the mind while simultaneously exercising the muscles. The complete focus it requires turns practice into a form of meditation through movement. On a physical, muscular level, samurai sword practice can build strength and endurance and can burn calories, just like any other comparably sustained, rigorous form of exercise.

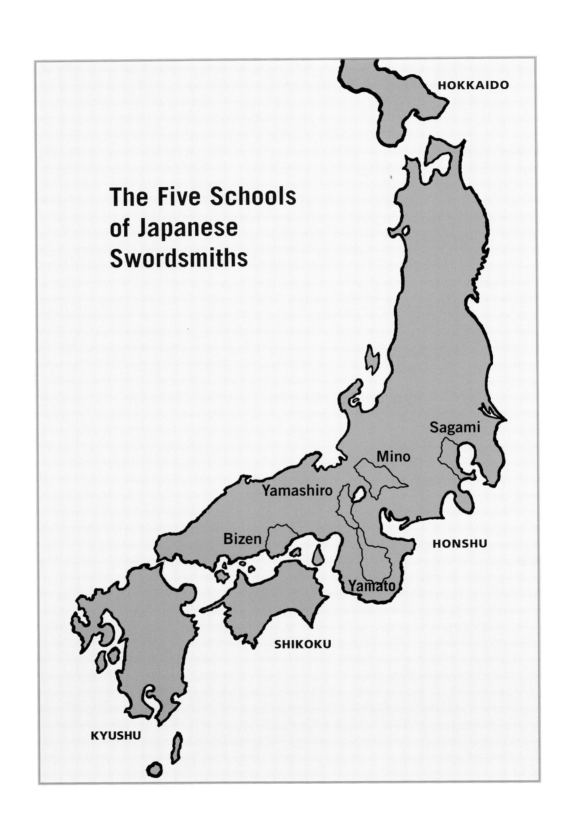

The Five Schools
of Japanese
Swordsmiths

HOKKAIDO

Sagami

Mino

Yamashiro

Bizen

HONSHU

Yamato

SHIKOKU

KYUSHU

Chapter 1

The History of the Samurai Sword

The samurai sword as we know it today evolved as a practical weapon used regularly in battle. As the needs of Japan's warriors changed and evolved over more than a thousand years of history, so too did their armaments. This development of the samurai sword is often organized into four key periods: *Chokuto*, or Ancient Sword; *Koto*, or Old Sword; *Shinto*, or New Sword; and *Shin-shinto*, or Modern Sword.

Although today the samurai sword is used for different purposes—for exercise and relaxation, for meditation and important lessons of discipline—understanding its history is an important part of understanding the modern methodology of its use.

CHOKUTO OR ANCIENT SWORD PERIOD

The birth of Japan, like the birth of the samurai sword, is shrouded in myth and legend. We begin our journey through Japanese history with a warrior named Jinmu, who, perhaps during Christ's lifetime, sailed from the Kyushu Islands to Honshu, the central and largest of the four main islands of Japan. Jinmu would become the first emperor of Japan, after defeating the hostile tribes inhabiting Honshu's Yamato Province.

Legend tells us that this brave man was endowed with "spirit from the gods." But even the gods couldn't bring stability to Japan: constant struggles for power and control of land would bring down emperor after emperor.

During the period extending through the ninth century of the Common Era, weapon making in Japan was based mostly on designs created by swordsmiths of Chinese origin and, to a lesser degree, craftsmen from Korea and Japan. The swords they created would likely have been of the Chokuto, straight-edge type, modeled after the one-handed *jien* ("sword," in Chinese) or *ken* (Japanese pronunciation), with straight, double-sided blades. In 645 CE, the Taika Reform established the supremacy of the imperial family, making the emperor the absolute ruler of all Japan. In 710, the capital of Japan was established in the Yamato Province at Nara, marking the beginning of the Nara period (710–784). Japanese nationalism slowly gathered momentum, setting the stage for a great leap in Japanese sword design.

According to legend, a swordsmith named Amakuni (circa 700 CE) observed scores of samurai he had outfitted returning from battle with broken blades. Saddened by the flaws in his work, he sought to produce a superior tool that would return unscathed from the heavy use typical during battle. Amakuni and his son prayed for spiritual guidance, disappeared into his shop, and emerged about a month later with superior ore and tempering methods that resulted in what would become known as the first "samurai swords." But new materials and methods were not Amakuni's only contribution to the development of the samurai sword: purportedly, he was the first to create the superior one-sided, curved *tachi* blade.

Parallel to the refinement of sword-making skills, a myriad of combat techniques proliferated from experience with the sword on the battlefield, as well as in individual duels between samurai who employed the grand weapon. Its arc shape not only gave it martial prowess in terms of sword strength, but also enabled its user to draw the weapon much more efficiently than the straight-edged type. With it, samurai could draw and fight at a moment's notice, unlike those armed with the older, long and clumsy straight blades. Amakuni's modification of the samurai sword was perfectly timed: With Japan's growing nationalism came the need for augmentation of samurai sword production, in order to meet the needs of the national army which defended the emperor against potential usurpers.

But this new blade was more than just a weapon—it was the hallmark of a growing warrior culture that would influence every factor of life in Japan for hundreds of years. Who could have imagined that this single accomplishment by one Japanese swordsmith and his son would be instrumental in elevating the perception of Japan in neighboring communities such as China and Korea and, most importantly, in the minds of the Japanese people, who had formerly perceived themselves as inferior to the Chinese across the sea?

KOTO OR OLD SWORD PERIOD

The samurai sword would only become more important during what is known as its Koto period (900–1530). Civil unrest was fostered by the extravagant habits of the Fujiwara clan, whose daughters married their way onto the throne of the imperial family. A period of lawlessness marked the end of their avaricious one-hundred-year reign, as their greed (rather than devotion to duty, the hallmark of more successful Japanese rulers) enabled the Minamoto and Taira samurai clans to usurp Fujiwara power and reestablish order. It was during this time, about 200 years after Amakuni manufactured his samurai sword, that Yasutsuna, a swordsmith in Hoki Province, would "perfect" the sword. He utilized painstakingly chosen iron sand and ore, incorporating high-heat tempering techniques that became the staple method of producing samurai swords.

Another important aspect of sword making during this period was the Five Schools, organized groups of samurai sword craftsmen that filled the constantly changing needs of the government, as power in Japan changed hands and the capital moved around the country. The Koto period saw the highest volume of samurai sword production in Japanese history, and the swordsmiths of the Five Schools, each based in its own province—Yamashiro, Sagami, Yamato, Bizen, and Mino—produced 80 percent of them, some of which were purportedly the finest samurai swords ever crafted.

Yamashiro, the earliest of the Five Schools, established itself in Yamashiro Province, in the capital at Heian (present day Kyoto), and became the local weapon supplier for the imperial government while its leadership remained there. As with the other schools of samurai sword manufacture, an abundance of high-quality iron ore, iron sand, and nearby water was an important deciding factor in the location of this school.

In 1192, the Minamoto clan took full control of the government, and the capital was moved to Kamakura in Sagami Province. The Sagami, or Shoshu, School established itself in response to this move, and the Yamato, Bizen, and Mino Schools came about to meet the demands of samurai in other regions.

Nationwide, a new samurai class was born when the Minamotos became the first to establish a feudal system of government, or shogunate, with a military style of leadership. This differed from despotic rule by a single emperor; the shogunate was a hierarchy in which regional feudal lords called *daimyo* answered to the *shogun* (military leader), and the samurai, highly trained and loyal warriors, served the interests of the daimyos.

A samurai went to exhaustive lengths to protect his master's honor, as well as his own, while at all times thinking of the "spirit of Japan," which made up the fabric of his being. As a consequence of his belief that his service to his nation was tantamount to his duty to his daimyo, he outwardly manifested unceasing respect, courtesy, and justice in the presence of the people of his nation. The samurai took their role as protector so seriously that when they considered themselves to have been shamed or to have failed at some task, they committed ritual suicide (*seppuku*).

Bitter infighting within the Minamoto family resulted in the death of Japan's first shogun, Minamoto Yoritomo. Yoritomo's widow, Hojo Masako, enabled the Hojo family to rise to power in the Kamakura-based leadership. Then in 1274 and 1281, the Mongols attacked Japan, creating a national emergency. This crisis prompted the Sagami School—whose craftsmanship was a blend of the Yamato, Yamashiro, and Bizen manufacturing techniques—to pursue rigorous samurai sword production, to defend the nation by serving the needs of the Kamakura government, which was located in their province. Fortuitously, the Mongols would be thwarted by a combination of the samurai and what was perceived to be help from the spirits—typhoons that struck to the advantage of the Japanese during each invasion, leading them to victory. On the domestic front, the shogun system had begun to fail. The quasi-military leadership, including officials who were more like civil servants than strong warriors, was weakened by the expense of defending the country from the Mongols. This created an opportunity for Godaigo, a man of the imperial line, to enthrone himself as emperor and attempt to abandon the shogunate system.

Godaigo seized power with the support of a clan of samurai warriors called the Ashikaga, but they later betrayed him by reinstalling the shogunate and forming their own government in Kyoto. Emperor Godaigo fled to the Hill of Yoshino near Nara, from which he attempted to rule the nation. For the next forty-five years, there would be two imperial courts, resulting in a lack of centralized control that encouraged lawlessness. Land disputes and power struggles between feudal lords led the Japanese into a bleak era of warfare known as the Sengoku period (1467–1574). During this period of chaos and discord, a broader spectrum of the Japanese population came to use samurai swords, and the demand for them continued to be great. The upheaval of these dangerous times and the increased availability of the samurai sword gave rise to what would become a variety of different "ways" or ideologies about how to employ the weapon. And as the tactics and techniques of warfare evolved, the samurai sword's characteristics were modified in order to address the particular circumstances of the swordsmen.

SHINTO OR NEW SWORD PERIOD

Some minor alterations to the sword occurred as we proceed into the Shinto, or New Sword, period (1530–1867). The tachi (curved sword), developed during the Chokuto period, became outdated. A lengthy blade measuring up to four feet in length, the tachi had been worn with its cutting edge facing downward, suspended from the hip of the samurai by a rope that was threaded through two rings on the scabbard. The revised version's blade length was shortened, resulting in a blade only two feet long, that would be carried fastened to the user's left hip by a sash, with the cutting edge of the blade facing upward. According to some sources, this new kind of sword was the first to be called a *katana* (single cutting edge). The katana enabled the samurai to draw the sword at a moment's notice and greatly influenced other aspects of samurai sword technique. Most of the iai-jutsu (sword-drawing) techniques described in this book came about as a result of this important physical modification of the weapon.

Some warriors of the era wore two samurai swords affixed by a sash at the side of the body, which were together known as *daisho*. These might have been composed of a katana or *daito* (long samurai swords) and *wakizashi* or *shoto* (short samurai swords), both seated on the left side at the hip. The shorter sword was considered an auxiliary to be used in tandem with the longer one, as a "back-up" in case of loss or damage to the primary blade, and even as an instrument to fall upon for suicide. (Today, this type of sword configuration is utilized in the more advanced levels of iai-jutsu; however, very few people ever train in this aspect.) A *tanto* (knife) was also worn, to be employed against an enemy of the samurai; it was also used if seppuku (ritual suicide) was necessary to preserve the honor of the samurai or his daimyo. In this case, another samurai would be appointed as the *kaishakunin*, to assist the samurai in seppuku by decapitating him, after he had cut himself across the abdomen.

Seppuku was just one of many ritualized traditions in the samurai's strict moral code of honor, known as *bushido*, or "way of the warrior." This code was to be tested by Oda Nobunaga (1534–1582), a samurai and military general whose ruthless tactics would have been perceived by samurai of the time as dishonorable. They included employing muskets, making sneak attacks, and torturing captives—all violations against bushido, which demanded that the samurai act within specific parameters of fairness. There had been a slow decline in "martial etiquette" subsequent to the fall of the Minamotos, some of bushido's most dedicated proponents, but the chaotic Sengoku period in which Nobunaga lived would see its greatest decline. Nobunaga's unorthodox techniques may have been the cause of his demise; he was either killed or committed seppuku when one of his own generals, who was also a samurai, staged an overwhelming attack against him at a temple where he was staying the night.

Nobunaga had been on his way to help his ally, Toyotomi Hideyoshi, in an effort to overthrow a common rival when he came under attack. Upon hearing about Nobunaga's death, Hideyoshi continued to follow in his comrade's footsteps and conquered more territory. Hideyoshi would eventually reunify Japan from its divided, almost anarchistic state to end the Sengoku period before the close of the sixteenth century.

Hideyoshi's clan lost control of the nation to the Tokugawa samurai in the battle of Sekigahara in 1600. This battle marked a shift in power that would result in about 250 years of relative peace in Japan under the Tokugawa "dynasty."

Circa 1600, the head of the Tokugawa clan, Tokugawa Ieyasu, came into power and strengthened the shogunate by clearly defining distinctions between the classes. The resulting hierarchy imposed a rigid structure and enforced strict laws that applied separately to daimyos, samurai, farmers, artisans, and merchants (ordered by class, descending from the most to the least respected). During this period (the Edo period, 1600–1867), Japan looked inward, closing its borders to trade and influence from its neighbors. Aside from Ryukyu (the present-day Okinawa Prefecture), which was taken over by a small clan of Samurai sent by the Tokugawas, called the Shimazu, the shogunate ceased all attempts at conquest and expansion, and Japan became a relatively peaceful archipelago. This era brought about a decrease in demand for finely crafted samurai swords that were constructed to function well in combat. Thus, the sword-making techniques of the Five Schools became more and more antiquated, as an aesthetic component to the samurai sword rose in popularity.

However, with mounting commercial interests and industrialization spreading westward from the Americas and Europe, Japan's closed-door policy was fated to be ephemeral. Japan's technology was falling behind that of the rest of the world, which was beginning to industrialize. Once again, change would come from within when the Sotozama daimyos overthrew the Tokugawa dynasty, ending the shogunate forever and reestablishing an emperor as ruler, in 1868. With this new emperor came the end of the samurai sword's golden era.

SHIN-SHINTO OR MODERN SWORD PERIOD

The end of the shogunate, and the reestablishment of an emperor as ruler, set the stage for a new era. For the samurai, this was cemented in 1876 when Emperor Meiji (1868–1912) prohibited the wearing of samurai swords. Samurai were rendered powerless in the eyes of the new government, which was evolving into a more Westernized form of leadership that did not depend on a powerful warrior class. After the ascension of Emperor Meiji, the Shin-shinto, or Modern, period of the samurai sword began. Changing political circumstances caused the need for the samurai sword to wane dramatically, and the quality of the blades manufactured during this period couldn't be compared to that of the samurai swords produced by the Five Schools.

The last "mass production" (both metaphorically and literally) of samurai swords took place in preparation for World War II. Unlike in earlier eras, these swords were made in mechanized factories and inscribed with a cherry blossom on the tang to indicate the Showa era (1926–1989). The low-quality factory productions constructed in modern times were of the katana style.

Over time, the way of the samurai sword has always been changing and evolving: the popularity and availability of the sword fluctuated, battlefield experience revolutionized how samurai used it to fight, and modifications to the sword affected the circumstances of warfare. These changes have given rise to a proliferation of methods of using the samurai sword, which one might contend emanated either from the swords that were available or from the innovations of swordsmiths striving to satisfy the whims of the shogun, emperor, or daimyo, who requested such instruments to fortify their retainers.

In either case, the plethora of techniques successfully used in battle by the samurai became the foundation for the evolution of thousands of martial ryus, or "schools of thought," that would make up a category of martial arts that the Japanese would refer to as kobu-jutsu. In spite of the decline in samurai sword quality and the sweeping social changes that brought an end to the samurai class, the kobu-jutsu disciplines of ken-jutsu and iai-jutsu, which are based on the wisdom and tradition of the samurai, quietly survived through oral and gestural transmission, from teacher to student. These aspects of kobu-jutsu constitute the theme of my next discourse and are the hallmarks of this text.

Chapter 2

Iai-Jutsu and Ken-Jutsu

Subsequent to the era of the samurai, the art of the samurai sword has been divided into two categories: iai-jutsu and ken-jutsu.

Iai-jutsu or literally, "quick-draw art," is devoted to methods of drawing the samurai sword and returning it to its sheath, using the most economical movements possible. It evolved parallel to the evolution of the samurai sword and provided an indispensable, rapid, efficient system of response to imminent attack. The three integral facets of this art are called in Japanese *nuki-dashi* (draw), *chiburi* (deblood), and *noto* (sheathe).

In contrast to iai-jutsu is ken-jutsu, which refers to the myriad of cuts, parries, thrusts, and blocks that the samurai would use after his samurai sword had been unsheathed. Although both these disciplines use the samurai sword, they are generally considered to be two completely separate martial arts.

The evolution of the samurai sword allows us to infer that ken-jutsu must have been practiced long before the development of iai-jutsu. Because the early samurai sword blades and handles were too long and cumbersome to be drawn and sheathed quickly, they could not have been used for iai-jutsu. Thus, a bona fide series of techniques focusing on the fencing aspect of samurai sword use must have been created and refined very early on, making use of the tachi—the large, primitive two-handed sword used throughout the Chokuto period.

A key factor in the development of both these arts would have been the *kata,* or "contrived sequences of movements," which materialized as a product of profound reflection on technique and methodology by battle-seasoned samurai. These katas would be practiced at exhaustive length, conditioning the practitioner of iai-jutsu and ken-jutsu (an iai-jutsu and ken-jutsu *ka*, in Japanese) to naturally move efficiently with the samurai sword. Like real combat with the samurai sword, iai-jutsu and ken-jutsu katas very rarely amounted to more than a few movements in any single direction. This is because it merely took one or two blows from the razor-sharp blade to render a samurai lifeless. The experience and familiarity with the sword gained through repetition of these katas were vital to the success of samurai warriors. Regardless of the protection given by armor, one thrust with the samurai sword's *kissaki* (blade tip) or a single hew with the *monouchi* ("maximum strike"; the ideal blade area for use in striking) could frequently be fatal or cause dismemberment. Hence, kata practice would be embraced as a necessity by an iai-jutsu and ken-jutsu ka, in order to condition a young protégé to follow the "way" of the samurai sword—which demanded that the samurai sword be wielded with confidence, composure, and respect toward the people of Japan. In addition, it was a means by which the most skilled samurai might maintain his martial acuity during more peaceful times.

Both ken-jutsu katas and iai-jutsu katas, the prescribed sequences of movements that were part of these practices, were modeled after battle maneuvers. Although iai-jutsu katas could be practiced alone, ken-jutsu katas would most often be practiced by two ken-jutsu kas. Here, the second person would be an integral part of the equation necessary for the achievement of greater fencing aptitude. Once again, contrived practice yielded exceptional conditioning, resulting in masterful technique. In addition, samurai would practice *bogyo-waza* (defensive techniques), wherein the opponents would spar, acting spontaneously to measure their fighting abilities. Bogyo-waza could indeed become perilous if one lacked adequate control. It was, however, integral to the discipline, because it bore the closest resemblance to a real engagement.

All of these different elements come together in the unique ideology of each ryu, or school of thought, within iai-jutsu and ken-jutsu. One's ryu determines how the draw, cuts, deblooding, and sheathing orchestrate into one flowing movement.

Each ryu is also differentiated by other secondary characteristics, such as the procedure for entering and exiting the training area with the samurai sword, maintaining the sword by cleaning and preparing it for use, putting on and removing the training attire, inspecting another's weapon, properly setting the blade at the side, and tying the scabbard's *sageo* (rope) for use or storage. All of the aforementioned would be practiced piously by the iai-jutsu ka in a routine, ritualized manner referred to as saho (formal etiquette), which served to put the samurai in the bushi (warrior) frame of mind, to prepare himself for practice or real confrontation.

This history of, and contrast between, iai-jutsu and ken-jutsu lead us to Fukasa-Ryu iai-jutsu and ken-jutsu, the ryu detailed in this book.

FUKASA-RYU IAI-JUTSU AND KEN-JUTSU

The Fukasa-Ryu style of iai-jutsu and ken-jutsu is different from other ryu that enforce a separation between iai-jutsu and ken-jutsu. Here, we view and explore these two arts as complementary parts of a whole.

It is important to recognize that in each ryu there is what might be called a "tacit" set of parameters that constrain which samurai practices are classified as iai-jutsu and ken-jutsu. Although these two arts are inherently connected, most individual ryus are devoted to one of them at the expense of the other. In contrast, Fukasa-Ryu iai-jutsu and ken-jutsu incorporates each art symbiotically for the most efficient use of the samurai sword. The ryu, or philosophy, explains how the samurai sword is to be utilized in iai-jutsu and ken-jutsu and is merely a perspective from which to describe the most economical "way" to utilize the samurai sword, be it a tachi, katana, or wakizashi.

It may seem revolutionary to many, but this conception of iai-jutsu and ken-jutsu as a dyad is drawn from the long history and tradition of the samurai. Considering the circumstances under which iai-jutsu and ken-jutsu evolved—on the battlefield—they must profess practicality as their philosophical imperative, and the warrior's mind must yield to this notion at all times while employing the samurai sword. It therefore seems inconceivable that both skills are not elements of the same art—how could a samurai properly and efficiently use his sword, especially when working with a katana, without a comprehensive study of both arts? Fukasa-Ryu iai-jutsu and ken-jutsu respects that necessary relationship and certain reciprocity between the two arts.

In this book, we explore the underlying philosophy of Fukasa-Ryu iai-jutsu and ken-jutsu, which can be presented in a relatively straightforward manner, one befitting a samurai sword art. Fukasa-Ryu iai-jutsu and ken-jutsu is the holistic methodology of using the samurai sword, requiring a resolute mind, a command of practical techniques useful in warfare, and a strategy that incorporates yin and yang in every movement through a balanced use of defense and offense. The synergism between each ingredient of this straightforward "way" will create a masterful user of the samurai sword.

Chapter 3

Knowing the Sword

To "know" one's samurai sword can be understood in two different ways. On a philosophical, theoretical level, knowing one's sword means to merge with one's sword as if it were an extension of one's own body. Via regular conditioning, consisting of katas and free-form practice, the samurai swordsman begins to merge with his sword. The sword responds to the swordsman in a manner similar to that in which the limbs of the body move, with almost no conscious effort. This level of instantaneous and unthinking action is commonly referred to as *mushin* ("no-mindedness"). To know the samurai sword in this way reflects mastery of the samurai sword art.

Another way in which one can know the samurai sword is to consider how we relate to it as a tool, on the physical level. In this respect, we become acquainted with the samurai sword as we become acquainted with any other device that has utilitarian value for us. Knowing the physical characteristics of the samurai sword allows us to exploit it, maintain it, and repair it when necessary—an imperative for the bushi in any era. As with any new relationship (human or material), I advocate getting acquainted with the subject prior to practice. Thus, samurai sword nomenclature and maintenance are prerequisites for coming to know the sword.

The Parts of the Samurai Sword

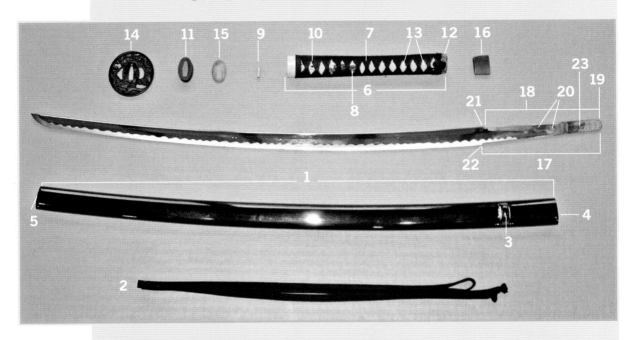

KATANA NOMENCLATURE

1.	Saya	Scabbard
2.	Sageo	Rope
3.	Kurigata	Knob that holds the sageo (2)
4.	Koiguchi	Open end (mouth) of the saya (1)
5.	Kojiri	The butt cap of the saya (1)
6.	Tsuka	Hilt
7.	Tsuka-ito	Cord wrapped around the tsuka (6)
8.	Menuki	Ornaments that enhance grip
9.	Mekugi	Tsuka (6) retaining (bamboo) peg
10.	Mekugi-ana	Peg hole in tsuka (6)
11.	Fuchi-gane	Cover at open end of tsuka (6)
12.	Kashira	Butt cap on end of tsuka (6)
13.	Samei	Ray skin that covers the wood of the tsuka (6) under the tsuka-ito (7)
14.	Tsuba	Hand guard
15.	Seppa	Washers protecting the tsuba (14) and fuchi-gane (11)
16.	Habaki	Collar for the blade

The Tang

17.	Nakago	Underside of tang (unsharpened metal area of the sword)
18.	Hitoe	Upper portion of tang
19.	Nakago-jiri	Butt of tang
20.	Mekugi-ana	Peg hole
21.	Mune-machi	Notch—merge of mune (30) and hitoe (18)
22.	Ha-machi	Notch—merge of ha (24) and nakago (17)
23.	Mei	Swordsmith's inscription

The Blade

24.	Ha	Cutting edge
25.	Hamon	Temper line
26.	Yakiba	Tempered portion of blade
27.	Jigane	Area between the hamon (25) and the shinogi (28)
28.	Shinogi	Longitudinal ridge located above the jigane (27)
29.	Shinogi-ji	Area located between the shinogi (27) and mune (30)
30.	Mune	Back of blade
31.	Hi	Blood-groove
32.	Kissaki	Upper portion of pointed blade-end
33.	Fukura	Cutting part of the kissaki (32)
34.	Boshi	Tempered part of the kissaki (32)
35.	Yokote	Latitudinal line that separates the ha (24) from the fukura (33)
36.	Mitsukado	Junction of the shinogi (24), ko-shinogi (38) and yokote (35)
37.	Monouchi	Maximum striking area of the ha (24)
38.	Ko-shinogi	Extension of the shinogi (28) beyond the yokote (35)

THE SWORD MAINTENANCE KIT

3.3

3.4

1. Uchiko	Powder hammer
2. Washi	Cleaning cloth
3. Mekuginuki	Small brass hammer
4. Oil cloth	For applying oil to the samurai sword
5. Choji oil	Oil for use with the samurai sword

An essential accompaniment to any samurai sword is the sword maintenance kit. It is a multipurpose tool that enables the user to clean the sword and dismantle it in a safe manner, without damaging the hardware or the sword's intricate components. Like an improperly maintained aircraft that might experience mechanical failure during flight and endanger the lives of its passengers, a samurai sword that is poorly maintained might lose its functionality and put its owner at risk. Hence, it was historically imperative for the samurai that his honor- and life-preserving sword be kept in an optimal working state. Neglecting to do so was a serious matter, because it could impair the samurai's performance and consequently result in a dishonorable death. Proper maintenance of the sword is no less important today. To ignore it is to invite serious physical injury.

MAINTENANCE AND REPAIR GUIDELINES

The following are guidelines for regular maintenance of the samurai sword. As a general rule, before and after every use, perform these procedures in order to achieve maximum functionality and longevity of the sword.

Prior to its use, the samurai sword must be lubricated with a small amount of choji oil, creating a light film along the sides and top (*mune*) of the blunted portion of the blade. This will allow smooth entry into and out of the scabbard (*saya*) during sword draws and sheathings. Additionally, oil is frequently applied for long-term storage of the blade, to prevent rust. However, caution should be observed, as oil can cause the inside of a wooden scabbard to swell, which in time might prevent it from holding the sword securely. Depending upon the type of metal from which your blade is constructed, it may not be necessary to apply oil subsequent to every use (assuming that you have properly cleaned the blade).

PREPARATION FOR OIL APPLICATION

From *seiza* (a seated position with feet behind the buttocks), the samurai sword is raised in front of the body, above head level, with the left hand on the saya and the right hand on the *tsuka* (hilt), all the way up to the *tsuba* (hand guard). Carefully remove the saya downward, at about a 45-degree angle, by your left hand, keeping the *ha* (cutting edge) vertical (see Figure 3.5). Next, set the saya in front of you, diagonally to the left. Place the sword, with its kissaki (blade tip) on top of the saya between the *kurigata*

3.5

3.6

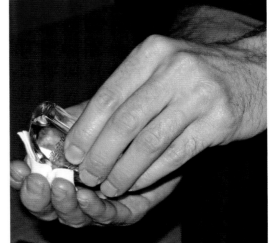

3.7

3.8

3.9

(the loop on the scabbard holding the rope) and *koiguchi* (the mouth of the scabbard), to the front, diagonally to the right, with the cutting edge facing the body (3.6). The sword and scabbard will appear to "envelop" you, preventing anyone walking close to or around you from inadvertently being cut (if they should step too close). The sword maintenance kit should now be lying on the floor just below the tsuka. In anticipation of use, moisten the oil rag with choji oil (3.7), and place it on top of the cleaning kit (affording easy access for use). Then lift the samurai sword by slowly grasping the tsuka with the right hand, and turning the ha away from the body (3.8). Next, carefully transfer the sword to the left hand (3.9), in order to free the right hand for an application of oil. At this point, the sword is held in the left hand, as vertical as possible, with a pre-oiled cloth available to the right side of the body, ready for use.

APPLYING THE OIL

3.10

3.11

Oil is applied by placing a small oil cloth on the side of the blade at the *habaki* (the collar above the tsuba) (3.10). Using the index and middle fingers as a guide, move the cloth along the blade's entire length, all the way to the end of the kissaki (3.11). (Keep in mind that the ha should *always* be pointed away from the body, never toward yourself.) Next, steer the cloth around the backside of the kissaki (3.12), and come down the opposite side of the blade until you reach the other side of the habaki (3.13). Last, slide the cloth onto the mune, grasp it more firmly with the thumb and two original fingers (3.14), and then slide it along the mune

3.12

(3.15), using the *hi* (blood groove) to keep the movement steady as you make your last application. Once again, finish at the kissaki. Immediately, drop the cloth onto the top of the sword maintenance kit and pass the tsuka back to your right hand, so the saya can sheathe the blade in the manner in which it was unsheathed (3.16, 3.17).

3.13

3.14

3.15

3.16

3.17

3.18

Afterward, place the sword horizontally to the front, with the tsuka to the right, and the cutting edge (inside the scabbard) toward the body. The sageo (rope) should run down the underside of the saya and come around the *kojiri* (the end of the scabbard) to the topside of the saya. Finally, the oil cloth is placed back into the sword maintenance kit, and the kit is moved back under the tsuka, its location prior to oiling (3.18).

PROCEDURES FOR SHORT- AND LONG-TERM STORAGE

As described above, while assuming seiza, the sword is held in front of the body in the exact manner as it would be for oiling. Now, however, the washi (large cleaning cloth) should lie easily accessible, so that it can be used to wipe the blade free of the choji oil and any residue that may have sullied the blade from samurai sword use. Even the oils from human skin can deteriorate the blade, shortening its life significantly.

The proper method of cleaning the residues from the blade, after the tsuka has been placed in the left hand, is to first wipe the entire surface of the blade, holding the washi in the right hand. This cloth is to be folded large enough so that it can "sandwich" both sides of the blade, including the mune, where the most pressure is applied during cleaning. The ha is never to come in direct contact with the cloth, as this could place the fingers in danger of being cut. Beginning at the habaki (3.19), move the cloth up the length of the sword to the kissaki, using a firm grip (3.20), then remove the cloth

3.19

3.20

3.21

3.22

3.23

3.24

3.25

3.26

from the sword, and repeat the wiping process as many more times as necessary to rid the blade of all visible residue. Now set the washi atop the open maintenance kit, and use the uchiko (powder hammer) to eliminate any microscopic traces of oil. Powder is correctly applied by gently hammering (in this order) the left side (3.21), right side (3.22), and back side (mune) of the blade (3.23). Keep in mind that the blade must stay in the left hand, and that the ha should never be turned toward the body. Following the completion of this process, replace the uchiko by the washi (in the right hand), and wipe the blade in the same way as just prior to powdering. After the blade appears to be clean, it should be once again returned to its scabbard (3.24, 3.25) and placed horizontally to the front of the body (3.26). If the sword will be stored in a humid environment, it is highly recommended that the blade be re-oiled to eliminate any moisture, which might rust the blade. However, this is usually not necessary if the blade is regularly used and stored indoors in an air-conditioned space. This procedure should be followed no matter how long your sword will be out of use—whether it is a period of a few days or many weeks.

DISMANTLING THE SAMURAI SWORD

As a general rule, I do not advocate disassembling a new samurai sword. A user will find that a new samurai sword's components are fitted tightly and are cumbersome to take apart. However, it may be necessary to dismantle the sword if the hilt or some of its other components seem loose or are in disrepair. I do condone and recommend dismantling the tsuka to inspect the *mei* (swordsmith's inscription) on a samurai sword that appears to be an antique. Bear in mind that a samurai sword manufactured in any era might have an inscription on its tang. And the mere presence of an inscription isn't necessarily indicative that a sword has great monetary value.

3.27

3.28

Whatever the purpose, disassembly is as simple as using the pointed end of the *mekuginuki* (small brass hammer) to push the *mekugi* (small bamboo peg) out of the side of the tsuka (3.27). After doing this, you'll find that this single piece of bamboo bears the burden of holding the hilt to the tang. If the mekugi refuses to move, I suggest hammering the topside of the tsuka (the side that covers the *hitoe*, or upper tang, below) with the right fist (3.28), while holding the end of the tsuka with the left hand. This usually loosens the handle slightly, allowing the mekugi to move more easily. The samurai sword can now be readily disassembled by sliding the tsuka, *seppa* (washers), tsuba, and habaki from the nakago (tang), leaving it exposed for inspection or repair (3.29, 3.30, 3.31, 3.32).

3.29

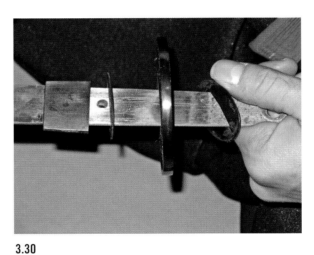

3.30

3.31

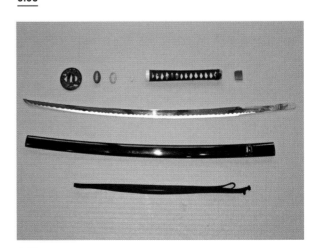

3.32

TYING THE SAGEO FOR SWORD STORAGE

Pick up the sheathed blade by placing the right hand under the saya and the right thumb on the tsuba (so as to prevent the sword from accidentally unsheathing). Lift the sword so that it leans on the kojiri (3.33). Be sure the sageo is pulled into two even pieces, with both ends hanging. Wedge the scabbard between the left index and middle fingers atop the kurigata (loop for the sageo on the scabbard) (3.34). Then, bring both halves of the sageo over the pointer finger (atop the kurigata) (3.34), and wind it around the back of the saya (3.35). With the right hand, fold the sageo into a loop, which will thread into the space taken up by the left index finger. Grasp the loop with the left index finger and thumb (3.36, 3.37), and pull the loop through (3.38). Be sure to tighten the sageo so that the loop doesn't become loose. Next, neatly fold the remaining sageo over the kurigata, creating an X-like pattern (3.39). Once again,

3.33

3.34

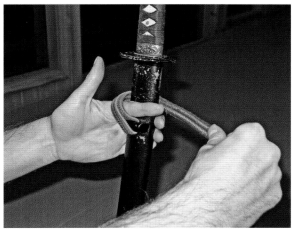

3.35

3.36

wedge the saya between the index and middle fingers, this time below the kurigata, and bring the sageo around the back of the saya (3.40), looping it and pulling it through (3.41). This should complete two horizontal loops (3.42) through which the remaining piece of sageo is to be threaded vertically (simply loop a portion of the remaining sageo, and thread it upward, starting through the bottom-most loop). Using the left thumb, push the sageo through both loops (3.43, 3.44), and then backtrack and tighten each component of the knot so that it can't easily become loosened (3.45, finished knot). Once this has been done, take one end of the sageo and thread it through any hole in the tsuba (3.46). Bring the other end over the outside of the tsuba (3.47), and tie both ends into a knot in order to prevent the samurai sword from unsheathing unexpectedly (3.48).

3.37

3.38

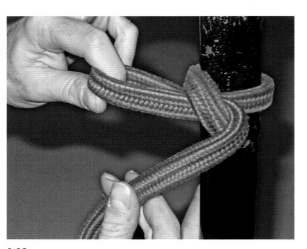

3.39

3.40

Place the samurai sword into the sword bag (3.49), and fasten it by folding the top of the bag over the tsuka and wrapping the cord around the overlap (passing the cord beneath itself and pulling it tightly) (3.50, 3.51, 3.52). Now, when the time comes to use the sword again, all that is required is to pull open bag's cord, open the knot on top of the tsuba, and pull straight down on the sageo and release the tie, a method unique to iai-jutsu.

3.41

3.42

3.43

3.44

3.45

3.46

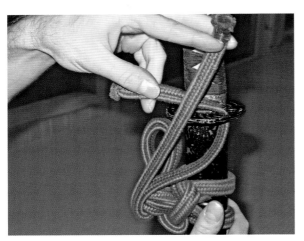

3.47

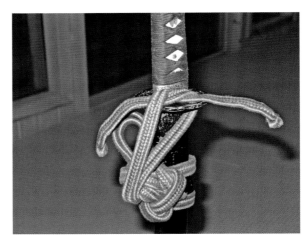

3.48

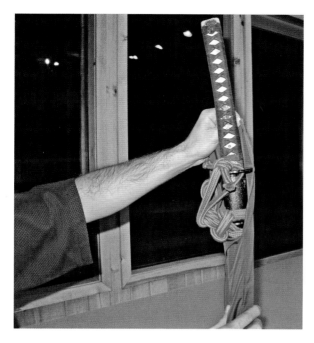

3.49

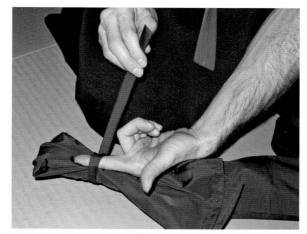

3.50

3.51

3.52

Chapter 4

Selecting the Right Equipment for Practice

Now that you understand the basics of the samurai sword, there are a few supplies that you will need in order to commence your training in iai-jutsu and ken-jutsu. You'll need a *bokken* (4.1, top—a wooden sword), a *suburito* (4.1, bottom—a heavy wooden sword), an *iaito* (an unsharpened metal practice sword with scabbard), a sword uniform (including belt), and a pair of kneepads if you aren't training on *tatame*, a matted surface.

In general, I prefer and recommend that my students purchase Japanese-made equipment whenever possible. While less expensive replicas of practice swords are available from other countries, the quality and balancing don't always match those of Japanese equipment.

You should purchase a bokken that can be used for both individual practice and practice with a partner during bogyo-waza. A bokken constructed of fine white oak, rather than the cheaper red oak, will not splinter as quickly and is more durable. However, if you do not plan to practice with a partner, the red oak might be satisfactory, as long as its finish is smooth. Always try to get a sense of if the balancing of the bokken feels properly weighted. This can be done most simply by gripping the tsuka just below the tsuba (with one hand) and turning the wrist to move the sword vertically in a counterclockwise fashion at the side of the body, to feel if the bokken moves lightly and almost effortlessly through the air. It's all subjective, but I recommend using this method to test any sword's balancing, regardless of whether it has a wooden or metal blade. It is important that the tsuba be large enough to cover your entire hand (as it grips the sword), be fitted securely to the bokken with a pseudo-habaki (rubber collar), and be constructed of a very durable plastic. Keep in mind that a well-made tsuba will protect your hands.

A suburito should have most of the same characteristics as a bokken. It will not, however, come with a tsuba, so you should not dare to use it for bogyo-waza with a partner. For this reason, you can get away with purchasing a less expensive red oak model, as seen in figure 4.1, although you might find that the white oak version has a lighter feel because it is more balanced. Suburitos are available in several different blade varieties. The most popular suburito can be found with a blade shape similar to that of a conventional samurai sword, while another style has a blade that is shaped like a four-inch by four-inch square piece of lumber (this tends to be heavier and swings with more wind resistance, creating a real challenge). Remember that the function of a suburito is to help the swordsperson develop strength, with the result of increased speed with a regular sword.

You will also need an iaito very soon after you begin your training in iai-jutsu because you need a scabbard from which to unsheathe the samurai sword. Depending upon your budget, there are many viable options for your purchase of a samurai sword with a metal blade, so you needn't feel overwhelmed by high start-up costs. The most economical choice would be to purchase a Japanese-made, aluminum alloy samurai sword with a wooden handle wrapped with a silk or cotton *ito* (handle wrap). This type of sword is not designed to be sharpened. Avoid a model that has a solid plastic handle below the ito, which could easily snap and injure you during use (swords of this kind are constructed to hang on the wall for aesthetic purposes). If the area just below the ito has a plastic layer instead of *samei* (ray skin), at least the core should be made of wood.

After my students have made a solid commitment to training in the samurai sword arts, I usually recommend that they purchase an iaito that is properly constructed for the regular wear and tear of practice. The blades of these Japanese-made iaitos are composed of relatively soft metals such as zinc or beryllium alloy, and are not constructed for cutting purposes. Such a blade is smooth, cannot be sharpened, and can be very easily bent if it strikes another surface. The tsuba usually comes with a smooth finish that is comfortable for the hand resting against it. I recommend, however, that one grip the sword by its tsuba before purchasing it, because sometimes the shape of the tsuba (in addition to its finish) can affect its comfort level. One can usually choose from a variety of different colors, paint finishes (on the saya), ornaments (on the hilt and pommel), and blade and handle lengths, with the latter given the highest priority.

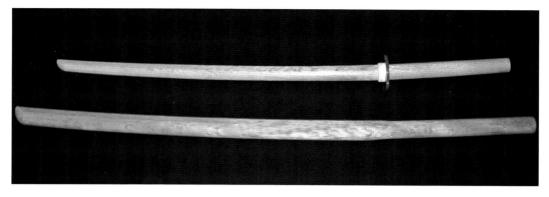

4.1

Beyond blade characteristics, everything else is just a matter of aesthetics or, in other words, personal preference.

To verify if a samurai sword or iaito is appropriately sized for you, grip the tsuka with the right hand just under the tsuba, and let the blade hang toward the ground at the right side of the body, with the cutting edge facing downward and the right arm hanging relaxed. The kissaki should be approximately two to three inches from the ground, which will permit easy unsheathing of the sword, while allowing maximum blade length to keep the opponent at bay.

I do not recommend investing in a sharpened (or dulled) katana for training as a novice, because you might be endangering yourself. If your heart is set on purchasing a katana for training purposes, wait until you can execute by touch each iai-jutsu technique with ease using an iaito, without needing to look at your sword. Only then should you dare to try using a sharpened katana.

Purchasing a katana for practice or for cutting *tatames* (common practice mats that simulate the thickness of the human neck) can be very costly. A good katana that has been handmade for cutting purposes is made of metals that have been folded and hammered under high temperatures, and its strength is derived from the tight layers and curvature of these metals. You'll find that there are many sources of mass-produced, machine-made katanas constructed of various steel types that will not necessarily hold up to regular use. Most samurai sword blades are neither durable nor sharp enough to cut, so they tend to bend and break on impact. To find a blade sturdy enough for regular use, search for a Japanese swordsmith whose skill has been passed down to him from a forefather who might have supplied samurai in the past. Since the purchase of a katana will require the outlay of a substantial sum of money, be sure to make a thorough inquiry about the swordsmith's lineage. Some practitioners may wish to purchase

<u>4.2</u>

additional swords, such as a *shoto iaito* (4.2, top—smaller, auxiliary practice sword) or wakizashi.

I recommend that young students of iai-jutsu and ken-jutsu purchase a shoto iaito, because the *daito iaito* (4.2, bottom—long sword) is usually too long and cumbersome for an adolescent to draw and cut with. In the samurai era, a young protégé (usually the son of a samurai) would use a wakizashi until he was of age and could wield the katana.

Use the same criteria to choose a shoto iaito and wakizashi as you would to purchase a daito iaito or katana. You will find that there aren't as many sources of good shoto iaitos and wakizashis as there are for daito iaitos and katanas, possibly due to the fact that there are very few practitioners of *nito-waza* (double-sword techniques). In Fukasa-Ryu iai-jutsu and ken-jutsu, nito-waza is taught only to students who reach the master levels of the system. Since there are, however, relatively few students who ever attain this level, and presuming that other samurai sword systems are set up in the same way, the demand for shoto iaito and wakizashi is far less than the demand for daito iaito and katana.

Chapter 5

Samurai Attire

In Fukasa-Ryu iai-jutsu and ken-jutsu, a violet *keikogi* (woven jacket) and black *hakama* (long skirt, with shorts beneath) are worn by students of the ryu. The fairly thick cotton weave of the keikogi acts as light armor against an unsharpened iaito, the metal samurai sword used in practice. It can also hold up to the moderate wear and tear characteristic of the sword disarming, throwing, and choking techniques connected with practice. The sleeve length of the keikogi should run about three-quarters of the way down the arm, ending between the elbow and the wristbone. Slightly shortened sleeves prevent the tsuka from getting caught in the cuff of the uniform, yet keep the swordsman's arms protected during training. This type of *uwagi* (sword jacket) is commonly worn by ken-jutsu kas of other ryus as well.

The hakama was once used by the samurai to conceal the arsenal of weapons they carried. Aside from the aesthetic element of the hakama, it helps keep the daisho (two samurai swords worn by some advanced practitioners, affixed by a sash at the side of the body) seated properly at the hip. It also allows the swordsman to move freely, without constricting the legs. The hakama is worn neatly pleated in the front, with open vents on its sides, so any and all weapons can be accessed.

The *iai obi* (sword sash) is worn to hold the samurai swords properly aligned. Especially in the higher-ranking techniques of the Fukasa-Ryu, where the daisho is utilized, the iai obi prevents either saya from shifting after the swords have been unsheathed (allowing one to quickly and safely return the blades to the right scabbard on the first attempt). In addition, the iai obi is wrapped many times around the waist of the swordsman, allowing him to utilize different layers to hold multiple swords in the same obi without the risk of damaging the swords' sayas by letting them continuously rub against one another.

In Fukasa-Ryu, the rank obi is worn outside the hakama, as opposed to below the hakama. This might be viewed as unconventional and deviating from traditional standards. This method has been adopted by the ryu, however, because it is difficult to identify one's rank when the rank obi is worn beneath the hakama. Thus, all elements of the uniform serve vital, functional purposes for the swordsman.

PUTTING ON THE KEIKOGI, HAKAMA, AND OBIS

THE KEIKOGI

The keikogi, as well as all other Japanese uwagis, is worn with the right lapel covered by the left side of the uniform. The Japanese associate life and vitality with the heart, which is located on the left side of the body. Accordingly, the left side of the uniform is always to be worn above the right side. Only the dead are clothed in the opposite fashion, with the right side of their apparel folded over the left, representing lifelessness.

After putting on the keikogi, fold the right side of the uniform so that it covers the front of the body. The left side is then folded tightly across to the right side of the body. Secure the keikogi by tying the cord that comes from the bottom right of the uniform

5.1

to its counterpart, which hangs from the vent of the left side of the uniform. The two cords, located about chest-level, are tied to keep the front of the uniform from opening up during training (5.1).

THE IAI OBI

The iai obi (5.2) is then secured tightly atop the keikogi, at the waist. Start by finding the area on the sash, close to either end, where its width narrows. Place either end just

5.2

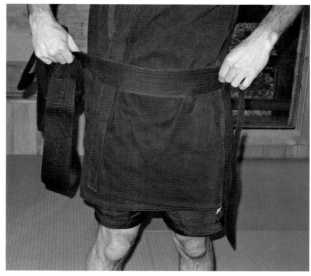

5.3

5.4

where the width of the sash widens, to the left side of the body, at the hip (5.3). Wrap the sash around the circumference of the body, starting around the front. Prevent the narrow area of the sash from becoming wrapped into the sash by holding it with the left thumb as you wrap (5.4). The sash is threaded around the body many times, until a piece measuring about the width of the body is left. At this point, the sash is folded in half (5.5), with the new end tucked deeply into the interior of the sash (5.6, 5.7), at the left side. The original narrow piece, now hanging over the whole sash (5.8), is looped vertically under and up through the sash (5.9, 5.10), at the left side. This secures the other end of the sash, which was just folded in half and tucked into the interior of the sash. The new end is then folded to the back, over the vertical loop of the original end, and the original end is folded downward, over this piece (5.11). Finish the square knot by taking the original end and threading it up through the new end (5.12, 5.13, 5.14). Turn the sash so that the knot is rotated all the way to the middle of the back of the body, out of the way (5.15, 5.16).

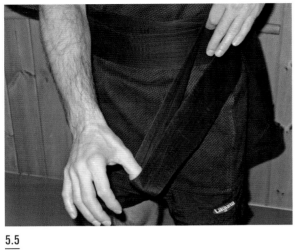

5.5

5.6

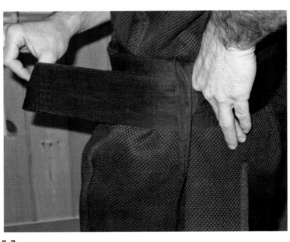

5.7

5.8

5.9

5.10

5.11

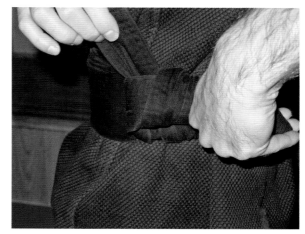

5.12

5.13

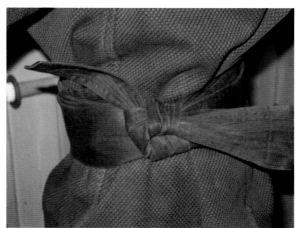

5.14

5.15

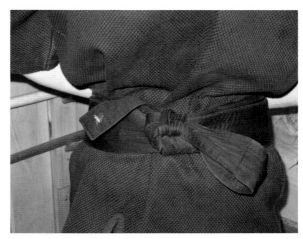

5.16

5.17

5.18

The Hakama

With both hands holding the thick drawstrings at the front of the hakama (5.17), step into it with both legs, and set the top part if its front onto the top of the iai obi (5.18). Wrap both ends of the drawstrings around the body (5.19), and bring the remainder to the front of the body (5.20, 5.21). Pull the drawstring in the right hand to the left side of the hip, positioning it over the other draw-string (5.22), and bring the lower

5.19

drawstring around the body once more (5.23), looping it over the upper drawstring, over and down the inside of the drawstrings at the left side of the hip (5.24, 5.25, 5.26). Before knotting both of the drawstrings together, fold the longer drawstring (if they are unequal) into a loop (5.27, 5.28), evening the two, and then tie them into a knot (5.29, 5.30). Hold them together and tuck them deep inside the hakama (5.31), in such a way that only the knot is apparent at the left side of the hip (5.32).

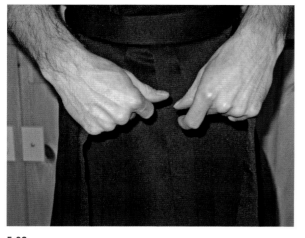

5.20

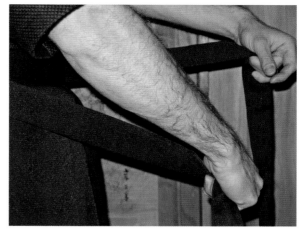

5.21

5.22

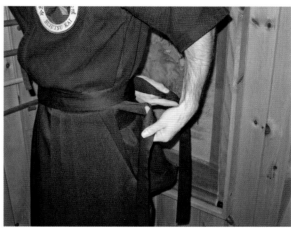

5.23

5.24

5.25

5.26

5.27

5.28

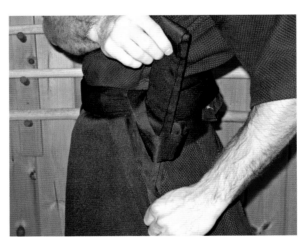

5.29

The back portion of the hakama is now seated atop the back of the iai obi. Bring the drawstrings extending from this section around to the sides of the body (5.33), thread them behind the drawstrings that have already been tied (5.34), and bring them to the front of the hakama, without wrapping them around the body. Twist both of the drawstrings into one another (5.35, 5.36), and then hold the drawstring in the left hand taut by grasping the other drawstrings from the front of the hakama at the left side (5.37). Use the right hand to wrap the other piece vertically, over and behind the multilayered drawstrings at the front of the hakama (5.38, 5.39). Continue to wrap it over and through once more in order to hold the knot at the front of the hakama (5.40). Holding the drawstring in the left hand, fold it neatly into even sections, approximately four inches in length, until it is completely folded into one thick piece

5.30

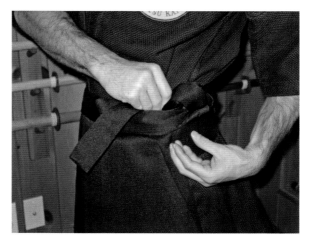

5.31

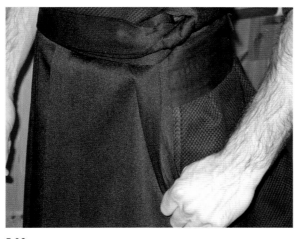

5.32

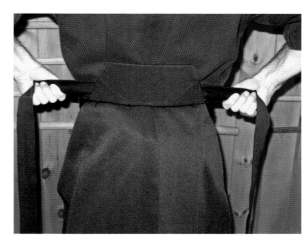

5.33

5.34

5.35

5.36

5.37

5.38

5.39

5.40

5.41

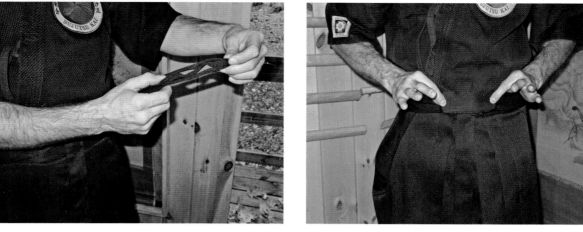

5.42

5.43

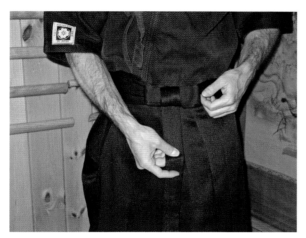

5.44

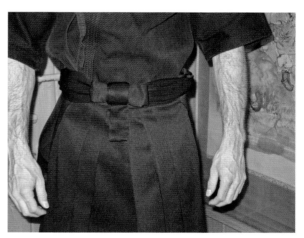

5.45

(5.41, 5.42). Place it horizontally above the knot at the front of the hakama (5.43). Finish by wrapping the remainder of the hanging drawstring over and behind the knot (5.44), and secure the bow until about two inches are left hanging down (5.45).

THE RANK OBI

The rank obi reflects the level of expertise that one has attained in iai-jutsu and ken-jutsu, and is a way to quickly identify the rank of a swordsman or martial artist. However, it is important to note that there are two different rank structures that are typically utilized by traditional martial arts of Japanese origin: The Kyu/Dan and the Menkyo rank systems. The Kyu/Dan rank structure was developed in the late 1800s by Jigoro Kano, founder of Kodokan Judo. This structure of student ranks (*kyu*) and

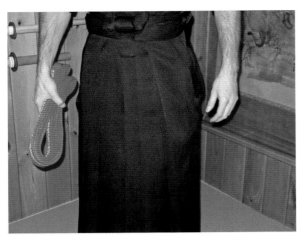

5.46

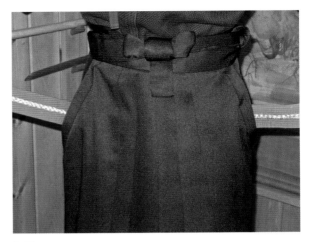

5.47

5.48

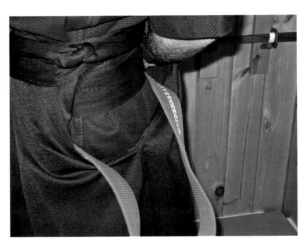

5.49

more advanced degrees (*dan*) allowed the deferentiation of students by a sash or belt worn in the dojo. Later, an extensive array of colored belts representing each level arose from this tradition. The older, less elaborate *Menkyo* ("license") rank system used licenses or written certificates to bequeath titles reflective of one's skill in a martial art.

The Fukasa-Ryu system of martial arts utilizes a creole of both rank structures. Iai-jutsu and ken-jutsu practitioners earn rank certificates with Menkyo rank titles for student and advanced levels and wear a belt that represents their attainment. This respects the old rank structure while enabling the easy identification of ranks within the dojo.

The rank obi (5.46) is put on by feeding one end through either vent of the hakama, around the front of the body (5.47, 5.48). It is then continued under the hakama,

5.50

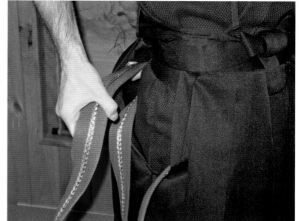

5.51

5.52

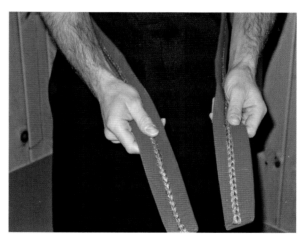

5.53

around the rear of the body (5.49), and out the back of the original side by the hip (5.50). Let the remaining portion of the belt hang suspended, and use caution not to let the end touch the ground, so as to demonstrate respect toward the discipline and rank structure. Next, take the other end of the belt and thread it through the vent (5.51), around the back of the hakama, and out the other side (5.52). Pull both ends to the front, and even them out (5.53). Bring one piece over (5.54), and wrap it under the other piece (5.55). Then neatly tie it into a knot just below the horizontal section of the bow at the front of the hakama (5.56, 5.57).

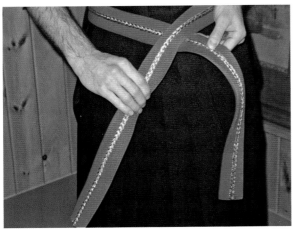

5.54

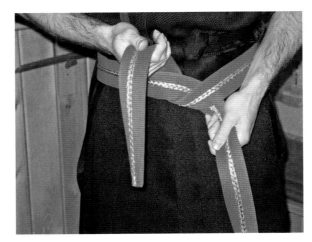

5.55

5.56

5.57

FOLDING THE UNIFORM FOR STORAGE AND TRAVEL

THE HAKAMA

Place the hakama on a flat surface, and bring both panels of the back side neatly together. Flip it over carefully, so the two rear panels are not disturbed. Arrange the pleats on the front side of the hakama, and pull taut and flatten all four pieces of the drawstrings (5.58). Position yourself in such a way that you are perpendicular to the hakama (it should be lying lengthwise in front of you, as in figure 5.59), and begin by folding the front of the hakama just beyond its last pleat on both ends (5.59). The fold should fall vertically in line with the sides of the hard back piece that supports the upper part of the back of the hakama, at the place where the two drawstrings emerge. Fold the length of the hakama into two equal pieces (5.60), so that it forms a square that is in

5.58

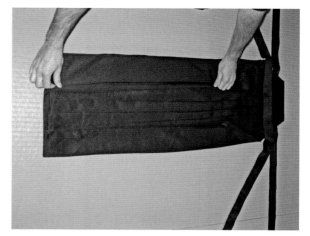
5.59

5.60

5.61

line with the drawstrings extending from its front and back upper sections (5.61). If necessary, adjust the direction of the hakama so that its top is pointed to the left, and the drawstrings run vertically at the left side of the body, with the hakama to the front. Take the closest drawstring from the front side of the hakama (not the piece connected to the back panel), and fold it to a size similar to the diagonal distance of the square fold (5.62). Layer the drawstring into even folds of this length, and then place it diagonally atop the hakama (5.63). Rotate the hakama in the opposite direction, and fold the other front drawstring in the same way, then lay it diagonally across the top of the hakama, creating an X (5.64). Turn the hakama back to

5.62

5.63

5.64

5.65

5.66

5.67

5.68

its original direction, with the top pointed to the left, and then grab the drawstring connected to the back side of the hakama and lay it neatly on top of the diagonal piece that you just folded (5.65). Wrap it over and under the X, to the left, where both pieces of the other drawstrings that were just folded are lying (5.66). Carefully fold it over itself diagonally, downward to the right (5.67), and wrap it under and up diagonally, upward to the left, securing it around the other drawstrings (5.68). Finish by placing its end through itself (5.69, 5.70), so that it lies diagonally downward, to the right (5.71). Pull the knot gently so that it is secured. Redirect the back of the hakama to the right (5.72), and follow these steps in the same fashion so that the appearance of the tie is replicated (5.73–5.79).

5.69

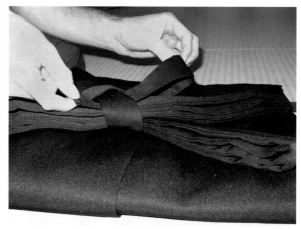

5.70

5.71

5.72

5.73

5.74

5.75

5.76

5.77

5.78

5.79

THE KEIKOGI

Lay the keikogi on a flat surface, with the arms outstretched, and the uniform folded at the front, with the left front panel covering the right (5.80). Fold the arms in half, so the cuff is in line with the vertical seam at the beginning of the upper arm (5.81). Then fold the arm in once more, so that the uniform is evenly folded, straight at the sides (5.82). The folded uniform is now in the shape of a square. Fold an entire side of the uniform,

5.80

5.81

5.82

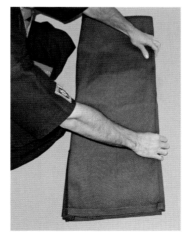

5.83

5.84

5.85

bisecting it, covering the front side of the uniform (5.83). Bisect it once more by folding it into a narrow unit (5.84). Finish by folding the long, narrow uniform in half (5.85).

COMBINING THE UNIFORM AND BELTS FOR TRANSPORT

Fold the hakama in half, so that its knots are protected within the fold (5.86). Fold the iai obi neatly, and place it atop the folded keikogi. Sandwich the iai obi by placing the hakama on top of the iai obi, with the back part of the hakama directly against the iai obi (5.87). Fold the rank obi into two equal halves, place it on a flat surface, and put the uniform, with the hakama on the bottom, on top of the middle of the rank obi (5.88). Wrap the rank obi around the uniform, and make a double knot on top of the keikogi, which is now lying on top of the hakama (5.89, 5.90). For easy transport, and to free hands for carrying samurai swords and accessories, slide your hand through the loop created by the keikogi and the rank obi, and slide the keikogi all the way up to the bicep (5.91).

5.86

5.87

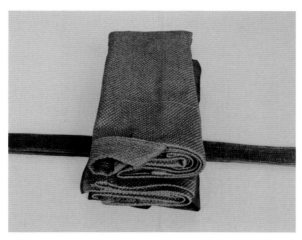

5.88

5.89

5.90

5.91

Chapter 6

Saho (Formal Etiquette)

It is my conviction that saho, or formal etiquette, is the epitome of kobu-jutsu, and the fundamental virtue that transforms mere martial practice into an art form. Saho provides us with a vital framework for understanding, learning, and benefiting from the martial arts that we practice. An absence of saho would render kobu-jutsu chaotic, "unsystematized," a conglomeration of random techniques that *might* fortuitously survive in a tenuous and crude existence. Therefore, saho should be practiced in conjunction with, and with as much intensity as, the physical movements of iai-jutsu and ken-jutsu.

ENTERING THE DOJO TRAINING SPACE

Barefoot, donning a uwagi (sword jacket) and shorts with a hakama (uniform skirt), iai obi (sword sash), and rank obi (regular belt) under the left arm, while holding the sword maintenance kit in the left hand, the student waits for acknowledgment from the headmaster of the *dojo* (practice hall or school for martial arts). The sheathed samurai sword is carried in the right hand (blade facing downward), with the tsuka locked tightly behind the forearm (while grasping the saya within its sword bag). Once the headmaster's acknowledgment has been received, the student bows deeply and enters the training area humbly (with chin hanging downward), walking toward the place where students line up prior to entering the tatame (matted area).

6.1

When the dojo is full, students stand in line according to rank, their apparel (hakama and obis) neatly lined up on the ground to their side (with rank obis on top of the iai obi, and hakama below). The line of students forms opposite the *shomen*, where the leader stands at the head of the dojo. As the *sempai* (most senior student) at the front of the line calls out, "*Kio-tsuke*" ("Attention!"), there is complete silence and absolutely no movement in the dojo. All students bear "unsleeved" swords in the right hand (with the ha facing downward and tsuka tight against the forearm). Sword maintenance kits lie on top of the samurai sword sleeves, grasped in each student's left hand (6.1).

The headmaster stands fully clothed, with samurai sword in the right or left hand (at his discretion), facing the students with his sword sheathed. From the shomen, he gestures with a slight bow of the head (6.2), signaling each student to start the march around the perimeter of the dojo (6.3) to the station where he or she will prepare the samurai sword for use. Once they have arrived at their stations (6.4), the students should stand as still as statues, awaiting the command, "*Hiza-mazuku*" ("To the knee") from the sempai. At this point, all students drop onto the left knee and rest on the ball of the foot (6.5, 6.6). The dojo headmaster follows with, "*Hajame*" ("Begin"). This directive signals the commencement of the sword's preparation for use. The students then drop to seiza (6.7) and carefully place their samurai swords on the floor, horizontally in front of themselves (with the tsuka positioned to the right, and ha facing toward the student).

6.2

6.3

6.4

6.5

6.6

6.7

6.8

Next, the sword maintenance kit is set just below the tsuka (on the right side) on top of the sword bag. The sageo knot is untied from the tsuba, and the sword is held down with the right hand, while pulling both ends of the sageo together with the left hand (unknotting it from the saya). Still flat on the floor with the kurigata turned upward, the sword's sageo runs from the kurigata (in two equal lengths) along the bottom of the saya, around the kojiri, finishing on the topside of the saya (above the mune) (6.8). The swords are now ready to be prepared for use (refer to the sections "Preparation for Oil Application" and "Applying the Oil," in Chapter 3). If using a shoto (smaller, auxiliary sword) during training, place it above the daito (larger sword) when it is set upon the floor. Also, the shoto and daito should always be kept in the same hand while entering and exiting the dojo training space.

SUBSEQUENT TO OILING

After the sword cleaning kit has been placed in front of the body (against the wall, out of the way), the students return onto the left knee, signaling that they have finished preparing their swords for use. When the sempai observes that all students are on the left knee, he grabs his sageo, loops it three times around his pinky finger, and brings his sword to his right side. The students now imitate this behavior (6.9). When the

6.9

6.10

6.11

6.12

class is uniform, the sempai yells, "*Tatsu*" ("Stand up"), and the class stands up in place (6.10). The sempai now commands the students to face in the direction from which they came, by saying either "*Migi*" or "*Hidari*" ("Right" or "Left"), as appropriate (6.11, 6.12). The lowest-ranking student then proceeds first by retracing the way along the perimeter of the dojo to the original spot where his or her hakama and obis lie. This is done one by one, with each student cued to start walking when the swordsperson ahead makes the first 90-degree turn at a corner (allowing for plenty of space between students). Upon arrival at his or her original place, the student quickly picks up the hakama and obis, and tucks them neatly under the left arm. At this point, the students must wait for their classmates to line up and ready themselves for bow-in by the dojo headmaster.

BOW-IN ONTO THE TATAME

When the headmaster, standing at the shomen, observes all students to be properly lined up and ready, with their uniforms and swords in hand, he bows slightly, signaling the sempai to enter the training area (tatame). The teacher decides, at his or her discretion, how slowly or quickly to bow in each student. Respectfully, the students each turn to the headmaster and bow, before humbly walking onto the tatame, making their way (with chin down) toward their places in line.

Students are always to make sharp 90-degree turns (military style), keeping the back erect and swords tight to the hip and forearm. Students file into rows of equal number with equal spacing between persons, never walk in front of higher-ranking students, and always walk around the perimeter of the tatame. No rows are formed directly in front of the headmaster (this is extremely disrespectful). Students stand directly behind one

6.13

6.14

another, leaving at least four feet from the person in front of them (6.13). When all students have finished lining up in this fashion, the sempai commands, *"Ushiro aruku ni"* ("Two steps to the rear"), and the students simultaneously take two steps back, starting with the left foot. Next, the Headmaster commands, "Seiza," and all pupils drop straight down on both knees and carefully lay their samurai swords in front of them (horizontally, with the tsuka to the right and the ha toward themselves). They then place the hakama, with the rank obi lying horizontally on top, just below the tsuka (6.14).

PUTTING ON ATTIRE

When the headmaster is satisfied with his students' appearance, he directs the class to dress by saying, *"Taitsukiryu-o-hakama."* The class is now free to rise and dress in preparation for training (refer to the section "Putting on the Keikogi, Hakama, and Obis," in Chapter 5). After each student has finished dressing, they all stand patiently in *heisoku-dachi* (ready stance), awaiting orders (6.15). When everybody is standing in heisoku-dachi and the headmaster is ready to move on, he commands, "Seiza," and everyone once again drops directly to both knees. At this point, the sempai looks to be cued by the headmaster (usually by gesture) to guide the class through the rest of the bow-in process.

6.15

6.16

6.17

PRESENTATION OF THE SWORD

Immediately after the headmaster's approval, the sempai commands, "*Tate-no-katana*," ("Sword vertical"), signaling the students to bring their sword to the vertical position, while rising high onto the knees (6.16). At "Tatsu," the students spring off the knees to the standing position in unison (6.17). "*Naname-no-katana*" ("Sword diagonal"), and the students "present" the sword in the "port of arms" position, at a 45-degree angle in front of the body (6.18). "*Mai aruku ni*" instructs the students to take two full steps forward, starting with the right foot, then the left foot, then bringing both feet together. "Tate-no-katana" again: Move the sword back into the vertical position (6.19). "Hiza-mazuku": Shift forward, down to the left knee (6.20), and then gently place the sword horizontally to the front, with the tsuka to the right and ha toward the body (6.21). And last, "Seiza," signaling all students to drop to the knees (6.22). The sempai turns slightly on his knees toward

6.18

6.19

6.20

6.21

6.22

6.23

the headmaster, looks up at him, and says "*Sensei ni taishite no rei*" ("Bow with honor to the teacher"). The students simultaneously extend the right open hand (6.23), then left open hand (palms down), touching the index fingers and thumbs together, and bend forward for a deep bow, touching the forehead into the triangle created by the fingers and thumb (6.24). The headmaster reciprocates by bowing from the standing position. The students rise up slowly from the bow and straighten the back, once again assuming seiza (6.25).

HONORING THE SWORD

The sempai calls out, "Hiza-mazuku," and the students respond by rising onto the left knee (6.26). Next, the sempai follows by commanding the group to bow to their

6.24

6.25

6.26

6.27

samurai sword: "*Katana-ni-rei*" (an acknowledgment that it is a lethal tool that should be respected and not misused). Immediately, all students grasp the sword with the right hand around the saya, thumb around the tsuba (preventing the sword from inadvertently unsheathing). The left hand is then slid three-quarters of the way down the underside of the saya, with the sageo taut against it (the end of the sageo will naturally hang down beyond the left hand). After all students are holding the sword up in front of the face, the headmaster commands them to bow: "*Rei.*" The bow is executed by bringing the sword (whose ha was turned away from the swordsman when it was lifted in preparation for the bow) toward the forehead, as the swordsman's back is bent slightly forward, with the wrists rotating the ha upward (6.27). The elbows unbend, and, once again, the sword is in the sight of the swordsman. The headmaster then says, "*Hai*" ("Yes"), and the swords are placed horizontally on the tatame in front of the

6.28

6.29

6.30

6.31

students (with the ha facing the body) (6.28), as the sageo is neatened around the kojiri of the saya. After everyone has completed this, the sempai pops his hakama by hitting its hanging portion below the knee and moving it to the outside of the leg, so it sits neatly at his side. Everyone follows by settling into seiza (6.29). Once everyone is sitting and poised to continue, the headmaster gestures the sempai to proceed. The sempai calls out, "Hiza-mazuku" again (6.30), and the command to tie the sageo, "*Sageo musubi*," is given. The class now rotates the sword toward the body (turning the ha away from the body), and proceeds to tie two knots, using the two pieces of the sageo (6.31). (Each knot is to be tied three to four inches from each end, starting with the end closest to the kurigata.) This is done by pulling the sageo in such a way that each end is lined up, separating it into two even pieces (one on top of the other). Slide the bottom piece of the sageo between the left index and middle fingers. The other

6.32

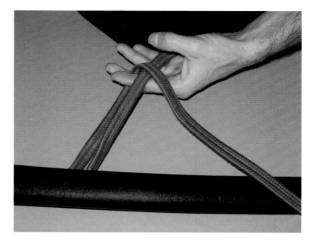

6.33

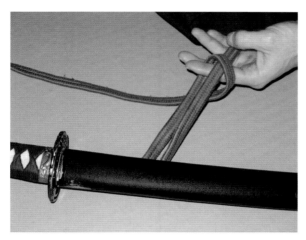

6.34

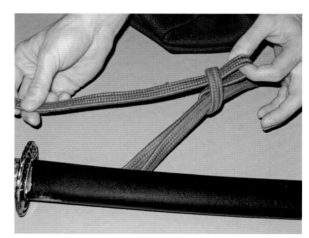

6.35

piece of the sageo should fall above the index finger, as in Figure 6.32. Using the right hand, bring the bottom piece of the sageo neatly over the upper half (6.33). Next, continue to wrap it down and around both halves (6.34). Finish the knot by pulling it through the space where the left index finger was (6.35). Once both knots are completed in this fashion, the sword is rotated forward, returning it to its original position (the sageo should run below the saya and up around the kojiri). Each class

6.36

6.37

member waits on the left knee until everyone has finished their ties (6.36).

When every student is poised to move on, the headmaster acknowledges this by signaling the return to seiza (6.37). He then cues the sempai to proceed with the same set of instructions in reverse order, with the result that all students return to the original position in which they stood after bowing in to the tatame. The sempai next issues the following directives: "Tate-no-katana" (6.38), "Tatsu"

6.38

6.39

6.40

6.41

(6.39), "Naname-no-katana" (6.40), "Ushiro aruku ni" ("Two steps back," starting with the left foot, then the right foot, ending with both feet together), "Tate-no-katana" (6.41) and "Hiza-mazuku," as all students drop back, down on the left knee (6.42), with sword in the vertical position. At this point, the sempai looks up at the headmaster, who commands, "*Taito*" ("Seat the sword"), with the students accomplishing this by letting go of the saya with the left hand and sliding the left thumb deep into the iai obi (6.43). The kojiri is next placed in the space provided by the left thumb (sandwiched between two pieces of the iai obi) (6.44), and the saya is fed through the sash by the pressure from the right hand, which is holding the saya (by the kurigata) and the tsuba (with the thumb). Once the sword is properly seated (6.45), coming through the vent on the left side of the hakama, the sageo is wrapped around the saya, and secured to the iai obi.

6.42

6.43

6.44

6.45

6.46

6.47

6.48

6.49

WRAPPING THE SAGEO

The sageo is wrapped once around the saya, just above the kurigata, in this fashion: First, the sageo hangs freely from the kurigata (6.46). Second, the sageo is set over the left wrist (by the right hand) (6.47), hanging over the left side of the wrist (6.48). Third, the sword is grasped by the right hand above the kurigata (on the saya), with the thumb on the tsuba for safety (6.49). Fourth, the left hand releases its hold of the saya, allowing the sageo to drop directly onto the saya between the kurigata and the koiguchi, which now hangs over the left side. Fifth, the left hand again grasps the saya (this time on top of the sageo) (6.50), with the thumb securing the sword, relieving the right hand. Finally, the free end of the sageo (at its knot) is fed up into the iai obi, through the right vent of the hakama at the right hip (with the right hand) (6.51, 6.52, 6.53). This knot is to be pulled downward, tightly against the top part of the iai obi, allowing one to move the scabbard more freely during practice. At this

6.50

6.51

6.52

6.53

point, all students remain on the knee, with the left hand securing the sword (which, in its scabbard, should be seated deep in the iai obi) (6.54), awaiting the headmaster's command to stand, "Tatsu," and commence training (6.55, 6.56).

FINAL THOUGHTS REGARDING SAHO

While it is imperative that one regularly and piously adhere to the saho format as prescribed by the ryu, constraints related to the physical

6.54

6.55

6.56

training space might impose certain limitations. Keep in mind that iai-jutsu and ken-jutsu, unlike *budo* (the noncombative practice of martial arts), came about and were practiced by the samurai in a variety of environments outside the context of the dojo. The luxury of the ideal spatial orientation when lining up to enter the training area, kneeling down to prepare the swords for use, and filing in by rank order to honor the sword and headmaster might not be possible in your training accommodations, and the practice may need to be altered slightly. It is also important to recognize that many ryus evolved from the samurai traditions, yielding various protocols, each with different logic concerning how saho was to be conducted.

Chapter 7

Sword Holds

The modern practice and use of the samurai sword was not an abstract art born in a vacuum. Instead, it developed from the practical experiences of generations of warriors. It is particularly easy to see these historical underpinnings in two issues that concern today's practitioners: the manner in which one carries a sword and the method of displaying it.

The manner in which we present ourselves to the world very often speaks volumes about our character and intentions. The samurai lived and died by an uncompromising set of values, in a country where etiquette was of paramount importance. They attached much significance to their appearance, believing that there were often tacit implications in simple gestures or nuances of expression. A blatant disregard for, or failure to recognize and abide by, a Samurai's subtle warnings often resulted in physical retribution, with the intention of preserving honor from being blemished. It was thus essential for samurai (and those who came in contact with them) to have a profound understanding of how their actions and appearances might be perceived by other samurai. Perhaps the clearest indicator of a samurai's attitude was how he held his sword, arguably the greatest weapon at his disposal.

From our knowledge of Japanese history, we know that a samurai's work as a retainer for his lord could change, reflecting the whims of the shogunate. Therefore, a samurai may have found himself acting in many martial capacities. He could have been utilized as part of an army, waging war on the open battlefield, or as part of a smaller group fighting together for a collective cause, or in a patrol capacity, policing a community and enforcing the demands of his daimyo. Thus, if a samurai were to have the occasion to enter another's home, the consideration of whether to keep his katana by his side or give it to the host would have been, to his thinking, an important dilemma. Should he compromise his safety to prioritize proper etiquette in the home of another?

In another instance, where a samurai was policing a community, how should he present himself daily with his samurai sword? Should it be positioned aggressively, ready for imminent use, or should it be carried in a fashion indicating more trust of his environment (possibly with the intent of earning the confidence of the locals)?

Furthermore, samurai swords were sometimes inspected by others in order to appreciate their craftsmanship and look for notches on the mune of the blade, which were evidence of use in battle. (Samurai were known to file these small notches into the back of their blades to represent each death they inflicted with the sword, enabling them to keep an accurate count.) If a samurai were to be asked by one of his comrades, or even an enemy, to permit the inspection of his sword, how might he acquiesce and not make himself vulnerable to attack with his own weapon?

The following three scenarios will demonstrate the relevance of these considerations for modern students of iai-jutsu and ken-jutsu, and explain how they might be applied in the dojo, among others who uphold the samurai tradition within the dojo setting.

FIVE METHODS OF CARRYING THE SHEATHED KATANA

1. Certain Confrontation: Holding the katana in the left hand, with the ha pointed downward (7.1), is considered highly confrontational. The sword can be most easily drawn from this position, and in samurai times, it meant that the sword bearer was preparing for imminent attack. Should a student carry his sword in this way when entering or within the dojo (out of the context of practice), it will be perceived as disrespectful and distrusting.

7.1

2. Aggressive: Holding the katana in the left hand, with the ha pointed upward (7.2), is still considered confrontational, although not as aggressive as the first method. The sword can still be drawn, but the blade isn't positioned in an optimal direction to inflict maximum damage in an instant. This method of holding the sword is also unacceptable in the dojo, outside the context of practice.

3. Passive: Holding the katana in the right hand, with the ha pointed downward, does not imply an awareness of impending danger (7.3). It hints of trustfulness and reflects passivity. A samurai could have drawn his blade with his left hand, but this was uncommon. In the dojo, this is an acceptable manner of holding the samurai sword; it is not reflective, however, of deep respect and trust for the dojo.

4. Complete Trust: Holding the katana in the right hand, with the ha pointed upward, unequivocally implied a sense of trust to those who were in the presence of a samurai (7.4). This is also an acceptable method of carrying one's katana when entering or within the dojo; it demonstrates respect and trust.

5. Absolute Trust and Vulnerability: Holding the katana in the right hand, with the tsuka behind the forearm, and the ha positioned downward (7.5), would have been a foolish way for a samurai to behave in public. It could have put him at risk of being unable to access his weapon in a time of need, rendering him weaponless in the face of a sword-wielding samurai. This negligence could have been interpreted as disrespect for himself. Ironically, however, this is the

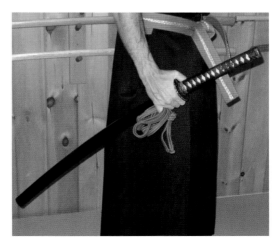

7.4

7.5

7.6

7.7

most respectful way of presenting oneself upon entering a dojo and the tatame (training area). This method reflects a profound trust and respect for the dojo and headmaster.

FIVE METHODS OF LAYING THE KATANA ON THE GROUND WHILE IN SEIZA

1. Awaiting Confrontation: The katana lies vertically to the left side, with the tsuka on top (tsuba lined up with the knee), and the ha facing away from the body (7.6). From this position, the katana can be easily and efficiently drawn, with little preparation. A samurai distrustful of his environment (possibly while eating) might have utilized this method of placing his sword by his side.

2. Aggressive: The katana lies vertically to the left side, with the tsuka on top (as in the previous method), and the ha facing toward the body (7.7). This might be interpreted as less aggressive than the prior method, though still indicative of some degree of distrust. The blade is still very easily drawn from this position, even though it might not be the most efficient way of seating it to the side.

3. Passive: The katana lies vertically to the right side, with the ha pointed away from the body (7.8). This is a fairly passive way for a samurai to have seated his sword beside himself, reflecting passivity to those in his presence.

4. Demonstrative of Trust: The katana lies vertically at the right side, with the ha pointed toward the body (7.9). This demonstrates respect for, and trust of, one's surroundings, whether the swordsman is a samurai or student in a dojo.

7.8

7.9

7.10

7.11

5. Complete Trust (in the dojo): The katana lies horizontally in front of the body, with the tsuka to the right, and the ha pointed toward the body (7.10). Placing the samurai sword to the front of the body in this manner demonstrates a complete trust of the environment. The ha is dangerously facing the body, making it easy for anyone to push the entire length of the ha against the swordsman, should the sword be picked up, sheathed or unsheathed, from this position (7.11). It should be noted, however, that some ryus view this sword placement as creating a barrier between the teacher and the student, thus creating a negative aura of disrespect in the dojo. This view is not congruent with the Fukasa-Ryu ideology.

SAMURAI SWORD INSPECTION

An acceptable method of samurai sword inspection must reduce the potential risk of injury (inflicted by the inspector) to the sword's owner. The swordsman interested in inspecting an individual's sword first politely asks if he may inspect the sword. He stands approximately six feet from the owner, as stepping too close might be interpreted as an aggressive act. Upon oral approval by the owner, the inspector bows in appreciation and expects a reciprocal bow from the owner (7.12). He then approaches within arm's length of the sword, as the sword's owner formally presents the sword, holding it with both hands in front of himself (7.13). In this position, the right hand of the owner holds the saya, with his thumb securing the tsuba, his left hand placed three-quarters of the way down the saya, and the ha facing himself. Next, the inspector

7.12

7.13

7.14

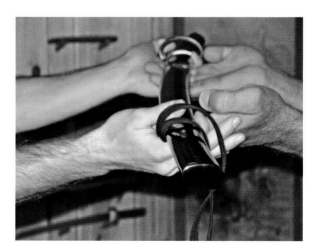

7.15

extends both of his hands toward the owner and places his fingertips under each of the owner's hands (7.14). The owner then rolls the samurai sword into the palms of the inspector, rotating the ha away from himself (7.15). Upon receipt of the sword, inspector immediately secures the tsuka with his thumb, assuming a similar grip to that of the owner, only using the opposite hands. The inspector now takes a small step back, holding the sword horizontally at shoulder level in front of his body (7.16). He can now request to look at the details of the tsuka and saya. Pending approval, he may scrutinize the sword by rotating it forward and backward, with the blade still sheathed (7.17). However, he is still forbidden to rotate the sword so that its ha (still sheathed) is turned beyond a 90-degree angle upward or downward, for this would make it possible for the sword to be used against the owner. Turning the sword beyond the allowed amount would surely lead to physical retaliation against the inspector by the sword's owner. At this point, the inspector may most respectfully ask to inspect the blade itself. If the owner disapproves of the request, the inspector immediately returns the sword to its owner by stepping forward and transferring the sword into the owner's outstretched hands (as it was rolled into the inspector's hands). However, if approval is given, the inspector slowly unsheathes a few inches of the ha, just beyond the habaki (keeping the ha turned in his direction, safeguarding the owner). The inspector then rotates the sword just as the scabbard was rotated, not exceeding a 90-degree angle upward or downward

7.16

7.17

7.18

7.19

7.20

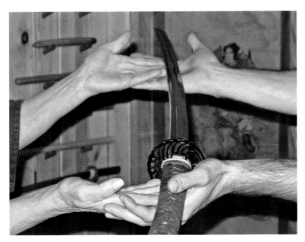

7.21

(7.18). At any time during this entire process, the owner should be able to retrieve his samurai sword immediately upon request. If the inspector asks to unsheathe the blade further, he does so only with the continued approval of the owner, and in very small increments. When the inspector is satisfied (or if the owner wants his sword back), he sheathes the blade, turns the ha toward himself, and presents the samurai sword in a frontal direction, at shoulder level. He then steps within arm's reach of the owner and bows in courtesy, with his arms outstretched and chin dropped slightly. The owner reaches out to receive the sword as previously described, and the ha is turned toward its owner as the sword is rotated into the owner's hands. The owner lowers his chin slightly (as a courtesy), and the inspector steps back to a safe distance, away from the owner.

In the dojo, the sword-transferring procedure described above is to be followed every time a sword is passed from one student to another, regardless of the circumstance. However, an unsheathed samurai sword must be most carefully transferred, because the blade can pose a significant danger to an individual's hands. Therefore, when handing an unsheathed blade to another swordsman—starting from *shizentai* (natural stance) position (7.19)—you must be certain that the sword's tsuka rests on your right palm, and that the side of the blade lies flat on your left palm (with the ha pointed toward yourself), while you keep your fingers motionless (7.20). Steadily bend your wrists forward, rolling the ha in an upward direction, so the sword rotates onto the receiver's outstretched palms,

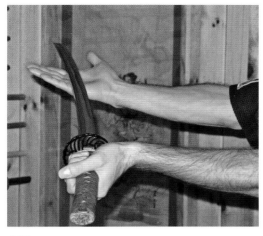

7.22

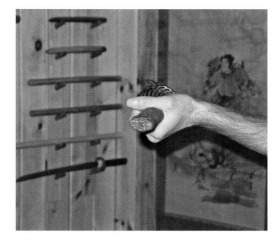

7.23

7.24

7.25

7.26

finishing with the ha facing away from yourself (7.21). The receiver immediately steps back to a safe distance to prepare to transfer the blade into his or her right hand (7.22). This is carried out by carefully sliding the left hand up to the tsuba, while the palm is still on the bottom side of the hilt. Then, the right hand drops away from the blade (7.23), allowing it to be rotated by the left hand, so that the kissaki moves clockwise 270 degrees to a vertical position (7.24, 7.25). Keeping the sword in a vertical position, at approximately a 45-degree angle from the left side of the body, the student bends the left wrist back to turn the ha away from the body. This is quickly followed by grasping the hilt with the right hand just below

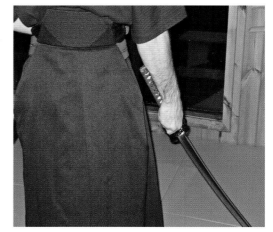

7.27   7.28

the left hand (7.26), in order to slide it upward, taking the place of the left hand
(7.27). The left hand releases the tsuka, as the right hand takes its position just below
the tsuba. As a precaution, the student must be sure to keep the ha directed away from
the body during this hand switch. Finally, the sword is moved to the right side of the
body while assuming *shizentai-dachi*, an "at ease" position (7.28), with the length of
the blade and ha directed toward the floor (refer to the section on "Kumai-Waza" in
Chapter 8, picture 8.6 for another illustration of this position).

Chapter 8

Ken-Jutsu

At this point, you might be wondering why I've chosen to introduce ken-jutsu (techniques for the unsheathed samurai sword) prior to the introduction of iai-jutsu (methods of drawing the sword), in view of the fact that one can't possibly "fence," or otherwise use the samurai sword, before unsheathing it from its scabbard. However, if we look carefully at the evolution of these two samurai sword arts and the way that the physical characteristics of the samurai sword changed over time (as discussed in Chapter 1), the reason for presenting these arts in this sequence becomes clear.

Chronologically, this order is clearly the most appropriate, because ken-jutsu must have developed prior to iai-jutsu. Early samurai swords had blade lengths that ranged from two to four feet, and they were typically used on battlefields by warriors who charged en masse, like soldiers with their bayonets in the American Civil War. Due to their cumbersome length, these early blades (tachi) were impractical as quick-drawing weapons. It was not until the development of the katana, hundreds of years later, that shorter, more easily maneuvered blades became the norm. The smaller size was a boon because this type of sword was developed, not for use on the battlefield, but instead for an environment where its mere presence at a samurai's side commanded respect and humility. This sword could be drawn in a blink of an eye if the need presented itself.

From a pedagogical perspective, it is advantageous to begin by first introducing ken-jutsu to the novice, due to the inherent complexity of iai-jutsu. The drawing techniques of iai-jutsu require the blending of many elements that eventually culminate in a smooth, flowing unsheathing. Executing this properly requires persistence, patience, and time. As an educator, I feel that it is important for a student to leave his or her first lesson feeling empowered, having gripped the tsuka correctly with both hands, assumed guard positions, and moved across the dojo with the proper footwork, while simultaneously cutting with the samurai sword. Iai-jutsu is usually a subject that I begin to touch upon during subsequent classes. For these same reasons, I have chosen to begin this discussion with ken-jutsu.

KEN-JUTSU: THE PRACTICE

As a prerequisite to ken-jutsu practice, the beginning student should know how to do two things: *te-moto* (properly grasping the tsuka with two hands), discussed below, and holding the unsheathed samurai sword at one's side in shizentai-dachi (waiting for direction by the headmaster), discussed in the previous chapter.

TE-MOTO (HAND POSITION)

Te-moto is correctly executed by grasping the tsuka with the right hand just below the tsuba. The middle, ring, and pinky fingers should grip tightly around the *tsuka-ito* (rope that covers the hilt) in an effort to touch the fingertips to the palm. In addition, the index finger and thumb should fit snugly around the tsuka, with the tip of the index finger lying comfortably on top of the end of the thumb (just below the end of the thumbnail) (8.1). The tsuba protects all the fingers of the right hand (including the thumb). It is critical that all digits be kept in place during practice, as the tsuba plays a major role during blocking. Next, the left hand grips the tsuka at the *kashira* (pommel), with the pinky finger curled below the kashira (8.2, 8.3), and the ring, middle, and index fingers grasping the lower end of the tsuka firmly. The left thumb presses on top of the side of the index finger, while the pinky finger exerts pressure upward, sandwiching the ring, middle, and index fingers.

DACHI-WAZA (STANCES)

Rei-nochi dachi (fencer's stance) is utilized in most ken-jutsu techniques. Usually this is done with the right foot forward, which is known as *migi rei-nochi dachi* (8.4). It is assumed from a "feet together" position, by bringing the left foot to the rear in a

8.1

8.2

8.3

left oblique direction (just enough that both knees can be bent comfortably). In this position, the right, front foot points directly frontward, and the back foot faces frontward, to the left, in an oblique direction. The body's weight is distributed unequally, with about sixty percent of the weight on the back leg and about forty percent on the front leg. The feet are positioned equally far from the center, both lengthwise and to the side.

The reverse stance, *hidari rei-nochi dachi,* is assumed in a similar fashion to migi rei-nochi dachi, with the difference being that the right foot is positioned to the rear and left foot remains at the front (8.5).

In ken-jutsu, migi rei-nochi dachi is most often used because the tsuka is almost always gripped with the right hand just below the tsuba (regardless of the swordsman's right or left-handedness). Posture allows one to move and redistribute the body weight to perform powerful cuts and blocks, and it must correlate with hand positioning for maximum efficacy. The feet follow the hands as they move from the forward to reverse positions,

8.4

8.5

working in tandem and creating an equilibrium that allows the practitioner to function efficiently with the samurai sword. Right or left hand dominance might superficially appear to be of significance in choosing the hip on which to seat one's sword, but this decision is actually determined by our body's anatomy, specifically the location of the heart—the most vital organ to be protected by the sword. Since the draw is the first line of defense against an incoming attack, to suspend the sheathed sword from the right side of the hip would be impractical and ineffective in guarding that life-sustaining organ.

KUMAI-WAZA (GUARD POSITIONS)

Shizentai (Natural Posture)

Shizentai, "natural posture," is a noncombative position that is assumed when the samurai sword is held naked, unsheathed. It is done facing forward with both legs spread approximately shoulders' width apart, with the knees slightly bent. The samurai sword is held by the right hand at the hip (with the blade downward, directly to the right side). The ha is directed downward, and the kissaki is close to, but not touching, the ground. The right arm hangs limp with its palm facing frontward, while the left hand grabs the saya with the index finger and thumb around the koiguchi (8.6).

The following kumai-waza (guard positions) are aggressive postures that poise the swordsman for combat:

Chuden Kumai (Center-Level Guard)

While in migi rei-nochi dachi, the swordsman wields the sword at approximately the level of the *hara* (lower abdominal cavity), with the kissaki pointed frontward (8.7).

8.6

Joden Kumai (Upper-Level Guard)

In migi rei-nochi dachi, the swordsman holds the sword over the head at a 45-degree angle. The elbows are slightly bent, and the left hand (on the pommel) is just overhead (8.8).

Gedan Kumai (Lower-Level Guard)

The chin is bent slightly downward (so the eyes can gaze down), and the sword is angled at an approximately 45-degree angle from the kissaki to the kashira (8.9). This position can be assumed after an opponent has fallen to the ground. (In a manner similar to chuden kumai in migi rei-nochi dachi, the tsuka is gripped around the region of the hara.)

Hasso-no Kumai (Vertical Guard)

In hidari rei-nochi dachi, the sword is gripped vertically at the right side of the head, with the tsuba at approximately ear-level. Both arms are held almost parallel to the ground with the elbows up, and the ha points directly to the swordsman's front, in a vertical position (8.10).

Waka-no Kumai (Side Guard)

Maintaining hidari rei-nochi dachi, the tsuka is situated to the right side of the body, at hip level. The sword is held back, diagonally to the right, with the kissaki hanging close to the floor, and the ha facing frontward (8.11). The sword is positioned for an *age-uchi* (diagonal, rising cut; see page 99 in Chapter 9), as well as other attacks.

8.7

8.8

8.9

8.10

Gyaku-no Kumai (Reverse Guard)

Assuming migi rei-nochi dachi, the tsuka is held to the left side of the body, at hip level, with the kissaki close to the ground, and the ha facing frontward. The left palm faces forward, with the thumb, index, and middle fingers gripping the tsuka. The ring and pinky fingers are located close to the remaining fingers, but cannot comfortably grip the tsuka, due to the reverse arm positioning (8.12).

8.11

8.12

Chapter 9

Suburi (Cutting)

Historically, mastery of precise and powerful cutting techniques was a vital part of samurai sword training. Like their predecessors, contemporary practitioners achieve cutting proficiency when they can synchronize breath control with complete focus of mind, while moving in a balanced stance and employing the totality of the body weight, resulting in directional acuity while executing a *suburi* (cut).

The ken-jutsu ka should keep in mind that a suburi can be effectively executed from a variety of stances and kumai-waza positions. With the exception of *nuki-uchi* ("jump cut"), which is usually executed from a natural position with the feet at about shoulders' width (when a samurai has been attacked from close range by surprise), I've chosen to demonstrate each cut from migi rei-nochi dachi, with the samurai sword held in the chuden kumai position. This is the most practical posture from which to cut during bogyo-waza, or the practice of defensive techniques, in Fukasa-Ryu ken-jutsu. In general, when one moves forward or backward with the sword (9.1), it is done by lifting the heel of the foot that is closest to the direction in which one desires to move. The body weight is then shifted off that foot slightly, enabling the foot to reach its destination by sliding lightly on its ball (9.2). Next, the other foot follows in the same direction, by lifting at the heel and sliding (9.3), with the objective of returning to the original stance at a new location (9.4). To protect the heart and allow the samurai sword to be held correctly, we want to move utilizing *tsugi-ashi*, "following-foot movements," keeping the right foot forward (9.1–9.4), rather than alternating footsteps.

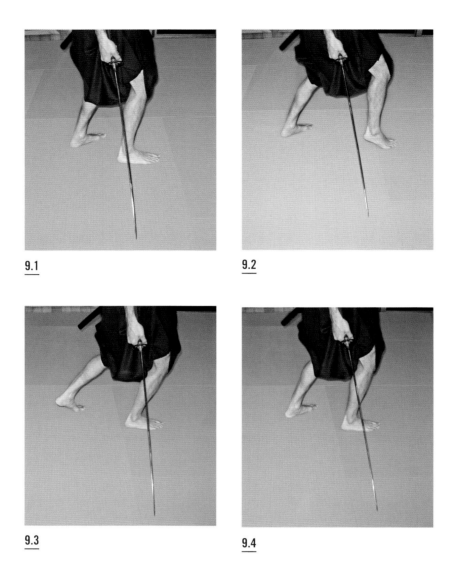

9.1   9.2

9.3   9.4

Enhanced by a balanced stance and a directional momentum (to the front, back, left, or right), cutting power is achieved through dropping the body weight by bending the knees, putting the force of the entire body behind the blow. Your arms mostly steer the sword, rather than acting as the source of power behind its motion. One who is mindful of this fact and applies it during practice will eventually harness the power needed to cut effectively.

SHOMEN-UCHI (VERTICAL HEAD CUT)

To execute *shomen-uchi* (9.5) from migi rei-nochi dachi (see page 84), the unsheathed blade is brought from chuden kumai to joden kumai (see page 87), while the right foot slides forward (9.6). The blade, pointing to the rear for greater momentum during the

9.5

9.6

9.7

9.8

cut, is cocked overhead. (The blade is not permitted to fall to a level below which it is parallel to the ground.) The back foot slides forward utilizing tsugi-ashi, reassuming migi rei-nochi dachi as the arms bring the blade downward to the front (9.7), moving all the way back to the chuden kumai position (9.8). Be aware that finishing the cut in chuden kumai (rather than ending in gedan kumai, which might give your opponent an opening to strike at you) is a safe way to cut with the sword, keeping an opponent at bay. A few subtle mechanics are involved in the execution of shomen-uchi: As the blade is swung in a downward direction, the swordsman's elbows, initially bent, finish in a completely straight, locked position. Additionally, at the cut's apex (above the head), the grip on the tsuka should begin to tighten, in a wringing motion for additional power, as the sword descends upon its target. (This wrist-twisting motion most closely resembles the wringing-out of a cloth.)

KUBI-UCHI (DIAGONAL NECK CUT)

If *kubi-uchi* is executed from migi rei-nochi dachi and chuden kumai (9.9), move the sword horizontally to the left, and bring the kissaki around to the rear, as the hands lift the tsuka over the left side of the head, while the right foot slides forward (9.10). Use caution not to drop the kissaki too low behind the head (keeping the kissaki from falling to neck level by holding the tsuka overhead, parallel to the ground) as the blade moves to the right side of the head, where it should rise to about a 45-degree angle (9.11) just before the downward motion of the cut. As the left foot simultaneously moves forward (to reassume migi rei-nochi dachi), the arms are moved diagonally downward to the left hip (9.12), exclusively by shoulder motion and with very little power stemming from the triceps. The cut finishes with the left hand against the left

9.9

9.10

9.11

9.12

9.13

9.14

hip and the kissaki close to the ground, facing frontward at an oblique angle to the left (9.13, 9.14). The ha faces diagonally downward to the left.

GYAKU KUBI-UCHI (DIAGONAL REVERSE NECK CUT)

Gyaku kubi-uchi is also executed from migi rei-nochi dachi and chuden kumai (9.15), employing the same footwork and circular motion as kubi-uchi. The kissaki, however, is moved horizontally from chuden kumai to the right (9.16). The tsuka is then brought over the head from the right to the left side (9.17) (crossing the arms into a reverse hold), resulting in a descending diagonal cut from left to right (9.18). At the finish, the tsuka rests at the right hip, at an oblique angle (9.19).

9.15

9.16

9.17

9.18

9.19

9.20

In both kubi-uchi and gyaku kubi-uchi, the cut moves diagonally from the neck area down through the opposite shoulder, exiting the body in the area approximating the armpit of the imagined opponent. It should be kept in mind that, historically, battle armor restricted the variety of effective cuts to those directed at areas of the body that were minimally protected to allow the limbs to function, such as the joints.

TOMOE-UCHI (HORIZONTAL STOMACH CUT)

Tomoe-uchi is executed from migi rei-nochi dachi and chuden kumai (9.20). The kissaki is moved horizontally to the left and then raised overhead (9.21, 9.22), from the left to right side, as the right foot slides forward. The kissaki is brought to the rear and the tsuka is lowered to hip level, at the right side of the body (9.23). The blade

9.21

9.22

9.23

9.24

9.25

9.26

9.27

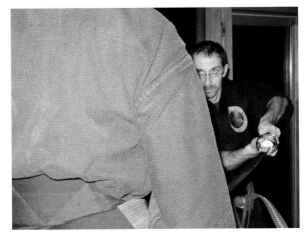

9.28

is now parallel to the ground, with the ha in the direction in which the sword is moving (9.24). The left foot slides forward, as the sword is brought horizontally from the right side of the body to the front of the left side of the hip (9.25, 9.26, 9.27). The bottom of the left wrist should be in contact with the left side of the hip at the finish of the cut, and the blade positioned straight to the front. If a samurai were facing an opponent in battle, this cut would have been directed to hit him horizontally at stomach level, moving from the right to the left side. The kissaki should not move any farther than the width of the imagined opponent's body (9.28). This is important because, historically, any extra motion that caused the blade to travel beyond the opponent's side might put the cutter at risk of retaliation. Therefore, use caution not to overcut.

GYAKU TOMOE-UCHI (REVERSE HORIZONTAL STOMACH CUT)

Gyaku tomoe-uchi utilizes the same footwork and kumai position—migi rei-nochi dachi and chuden kumai (9.29)—with the kissaki brought horizontally to the right (9.30), as in tomoe-uchi. The moves are executed in the opposite direction, however (9.31, 9.32), with the cut striking the imagined opponent horizontally, at stomach level, from left to right (9.33, 9.34). Caution should again be exercised to avoid overcutting.

NUKI-UCHI (JUMP CUT)

While nuki-uchi can be executed from migi rei-nochi dachi, it is not the most effective stance for practice against an imaginary opponent who makes a surprise attack at

9.29

9.30

9.31

9.32

9.33

9.34

a close range. However, the cut is executed in a similar manner as shomen-uchi, cutting vertically, down from the center of the head into the middle of the imagined opponent's body. This is accomplished by standing with both feet at approximately shoulders' width apart, in a manner similar to shizentai-dachi (9.35). The cut is executed by bending the knees deeply and springing upward (9.36, 9.37, 9.38). The blade, however, is taken around the left side of the body and behind the head (rather than straight up to joden kumai, as in shomen-uchi) (9.38). The combination of the circular momentum and gravity helps the cutter to hew down (9.39, 9.40), while landing (9.41) in a deep, wide posture (9.42), with both feet pointed in a forward direction. Be diligent in keeping the back erect throughout the entire cut. Land with the blade in chuden kumai and avoid overcutting.

9.35

9.36

9.37

9.38

9.39

9.40

9.41

9.42

AGE-UCHI (DIAGONAL RISING CUT)

Age-uchi is executed from migi rei-nochi dachi in chuden kumai (9.43). The kissaki is moved horizontally to the left as it travels to the rear, with the tsuka lifted overhead (9.44, 9.45), as in the other cutting techniques. This time, the tsuka is brought all the way around to the right hip (9.46), as the right foot slides forward, positioning the sword exactly as in waka-no kumai (see page 87) (9.47). Slide the left foot forward, as the arms draw the tsuka upward in a diagonal direction, from right to left (9.48). The left hand is on the end of the tsuka, in front of the left side of the head. Keep the right elbow locked. The ha is at an oblique angle in an upward, left direction, and the kissaki hangs beyond the tsuka, at about neck level (depending upon the size of the imagined opponent) (9.49).

9.43

9.44

9.45

9.46

9.47

9.48

9.49

GYAKU AGE-UCHI (REVERSE DIAGONAL RISING CUT)

Gyaku age-uchi is executed from migi rei-nochi dachi in chuden kumai (9.50), like age-uchi. However, the sword moves from chuden kumai in the opposite direction (9.51), from right to left over the head (9.52) into gyaku-no kumai (9.53, 9.54), resulting in a right, oblique-angle rising cut (9.55). At the conclusion of this cut, the arms are outstretched to the front of the right side of the head (in a reverse hold), and the back, left foot is turned slightly to the right, on the ball of the foot (9.56).

9.50

9.51

9.52

9.53

9.54

9.55

9.56

YOKUMEN-UCHI (SIDE OF THE HEAD CUT)

Yokumen-uchi is performed from migi rei-nochi dachi in chuden kumai (9.57). The kissaki is moved to the left, at neck level (9.58), around the back of the body, as the right foot slides forward. After the tsuka reaches the right side of the head, it is turned so that the ha is in the direction of the sword's movement (horizontally positioned to cut to the left) (9.59). The tsuka is then moved with both hands, at neck-level, with the blade parallel to the ground. The arms are extended to the front, across the full width of the body from right to left, as the left foot begins its journey forward (9.60). The blade finishes its movement with the ha pointed to the left, and the kissaki extended straight from the tsuka at the left (9.61).

9.57

9.58

9.59

9.60

9.61

9.62

GYAKU YOKUMEN-UCHI (REVERSE SIDE OF THE HEAD CUT)

Gyaku yokumen-uchi is executed in the same manner as yokumen-uchi. The movement of the arms, however, is reversed. As in gyaku age-uchi, the left foot turns on its ball as the cut is completed (9.62–9.66).

9.63

9.64

9.65

9.66

9.67

9.68

MAE-TSUKI (FRONT THRUST)

Mae-tsuki is executed from migi rei-nochi dachi in chuden kumai (9.67). The tsuka is lifted slightly with a vertical, circular motion and brought to the left side of the body (9.68, 9.69). The kissaki must continually point straight ahead. The right foot slides forward, while the tsuka of the sword descends back and down toward the hip. Next, the left foot slides forward, as the arms extend outward, eventually locking at the elbows, thrusting the kissaki through the abdominal region of the imagined opponent (9.70, 9.71). Keep the back straight during this thrust, and keep in mind that after the blade has been thrust into an imaginary opponent's body, it must be withdrawn. This is accomplished by first sliding back with the left foot, then with the right foot, as the tsuka is drawn back beyond the left hip, extricating the blade.

9.69

9.70

9.71

SASSE-UCHI (SUPPORTED CUT)

The *sasse-uchi* can be easily executed in vertical, horizontal, and diagonal directions. Prior to the cut, the ha is positioned in the proper cutting direction. The "supporting hand" is placed on the mune in a safe manner, with the fingers close together and the palm flexed tightly. Using a horizontal cut as a model, one can deduce how to execute the other variations.

From migi rei-nochi dachi and chuden kumai (9.72), the left hand releases the tsuka, and is positioned to the left of the body, with the palm open, and fingers pointed upward. The right wrist and hand, still grasping the tsuka, twist to the left, turning the palm downward, while directing the ha forward. The mune is brought to the left open palm, with the sword kept completely horizontal to the front of the body (9.73). The arms swing to the left side of the body as the right foot slides forward, cocking the blade back to the left side. Last, the left foot slides forward, as the right hand brings the tsuka across to the right side of the body (9.74), and the left hand pushes the mune to the right (9.75, 9.76, 9.77). Sasse-uchi is used most effectively at close range, where there is little space in which to move the weapon, and too little time to utilize a more penetrating big swing. It is important to note that on the battlefield, sasse-uchi was used to inflict superficial "flesh wounds" only. The mechanics of this type of cut make it difficult to generate enough power to cut successfully through muscle.

9.72

9.73

9.74

9.75

9.76

9.77

USHIRO-TSUKI (REAR THRUST)

Ushiro-tsuki is executed from migi-rei-nochi dachi and chuden kumai (9.78). The right hand is reversed by letting go of the tsuka, swiveling it toward the body, and then regrabbing it (9.79). The sword is rotated to the right hip, with the kissaki pointing to the rear. The forearm lies securely on top of the mune in order to stabilize the sword for the thrust to the rear (9.80). While looking over the right shoulder, slide the right foot back and thrust directly to the rear, keeping the blade parallel to the ground (9.81, 9.82). Remember, a samurai had to extricate his blade after thrusting it into the flesh of an opponent. Thus, it's important to pull the blade in the opposite direction of the thrust afterward, which would represent this.

9.78

9.79

9.80

9.81

9.82

Chapter 10

Uke-Waza
(Blocking and Evasive Techniques)

The ideal method of defense against an oncoming blade is "passive evasion," or merely moving out of its path, as opposed to "forceful resistance," executed via a block with the blade. This concept is rooted in history: to misuse or mishandle the samurai sword in a fashion that might compromise its functionality and longevity was an act of negligence that could have dire consequences. The samurai sword was regarded as the protector and primary life-sustaining tool of the samurai; although an inanimate object, it was accorded both respect and reverence. While death might certainly result from a poorly maintained weapon, a far worse consequence, in the view of the samurai, was the personal disgrace of failing in duty to one's lord or to the Japanese nation. To avoid such dishonor, painstaking effort was expended to protect the blade of the samurai sword from unnecessary disrepair or damage, so it could serve its user most efficaciously. In Fukasa-Ryu ken-jutsu, there are two phases of *uke-waza* "blade defense": blocking and evading.

Evasive ken-jutsu techniques were developed and employed to minimize sword-to-sword contact with an opponent's weapon and avoid damage to the samurai sword. There were, of course, instances when a samurai needed to ward off an attack by blocking it with his blade. Such a circumstance could arise if he was taken by surprise and could not react fast enough to evade his opponent's strike, or didn't have the space to shift out of harm's way. Even in this case, the samurai sword was used in a way that was least destructive to its ha. While executing a block against an opposing weapon, this is accomplished by turning the wrist slightly so the side of the blade, rather than the ha, is used to block. The angle at which the length of the blade is positioned at the moment of impact also greatly affects the durability of the blade. For example, blocking at 45-degree angles rather than positioning the blade straight minimizes the shock of inbound cuts, forcing an opponent's blade to slide off the area of impact. And last, if an evasion can be employed simultaneously with a blocking technique, the strike's damaging effect will surely be minimized.

EVASIVE TECHNIQUES

Ideal evasive techniques require that the swordsman move either straight forward, straight backward, or at an oblique angle to evade the strike of the opponent. Forward movement as an opponent cocks his sword for a cut is an offensive technique; movement straight backward allows an incoming cut to pass by, followed by swift, master-

ful retaliation. Movement at an oblique angle enables the swordsman to gain closer proximity (within cutting range) to the opponent. Examples are illustrated against the following strikes: shomen-uchi (10.1, 10.2), kubi-uchi (10.3, 10.4), tomoe-uchi (10.5, 10.6), mae-tsuki (10.7, 10.8, 10.9), age-uchi (10.10, 10.11) and yokumen-uchi (10.12).

10.1

10.2

10.3

10.4

10.5

10.6

10.7

10.8

10.9

10.10

10.11

10.12

10.13

BLOCKING TECHNIQUES

JODEN-UKE (UPPER-LEVEL BLOCK)

From waka-no kumai (10.13), with the left, front foot, slide forward at a left, oblique angle. At the same time, raise the tsuka from the right hip, diagonally across the front of the body, to the left side of the head. The blade hangs at a 45-degree angle, and the tsuba is positioned just beyond the left, uppermost area of the head (10.14). The wrists are bent slightly toward the body in order to keep the ha from becoming damaged by the impact.

This block can be used most effectively to defend against a shomen-uchi (10.15–10.16).

GYAKU JODEN-UKE (REVERSE UPPER-LEVEL BLOCK)

From gyaku-no kumai (10.17), with the right, front foot, slide forward at a right, oblique angle. At the same time, raise the tsuka from the left hip, diagonally across the front of the body, to the right side of the head. This block is positioned similar to joden-uke, but on the opposite side of the head, with the forearms crossed in the reverse position (10.18).

10.14

10.15

10.16

10.17

10.18

This block can also be used to defend against a shomen-uchi; however, it puts you at the other side of an opponent's body.

TSUBA-UKE (HAND GUARD BLOCK)

From migi rei-nochi dachi and chuden kumai, the right foot slides slightly forward according to the direction indicated by either the kubi-uchi or gyaku kubi-uchi. In the event that an opponent utilizes kubi-uchi, cutting diagonally from his right to left, shift the right foot forward to the left, at an oblique angle, into *zenkutsu-dachi* (locking the back leg and bending the front knee), and direct your blade upward approximately 45-degrees (from tsuka to kissaki) and to the left (10.19). Twist the wrists slightly to the right, enabling the side of your blade to make contact with the incoming strike, and pushing it aside. Permit the opponent's blade to fall all the way to the tsuba, on the

10.19

10.20

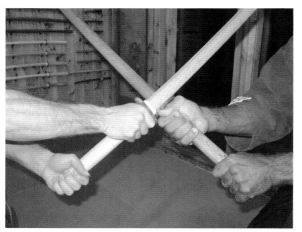

10.21

10.22

10.23

outside (left side) of your blade, shifting it left, out of harm's way (10.20, 10.21, 10.22).

When gyaku kubi-uchi is being used as an attack, shift the right foot slightly forward to the right, at an oblique angle (10.23), and execute the block in the same manner as above, compensating for the difference in direction (10.24). Afterward, you can follow up with a cut to the neck to finish the imaginary opponent (10.25), similar to the way it was demonstrated in the other direction.

10.24

10.25

CHUDEN-UKE (MIDDLE-LEVEL BLOCK)

From hasso-no kumai or chuden kumai, slide the right foot forward, at an oblique angle, in the direction from which the attack is coming. This block is executed against an incoming tomoe-uchi or gyaku tomoe-uchi. The blade is positioned at approximately a 45-degree angle, as the bent wrists rotate the ha slightly sideways to protect it, as in tsuba-uke. The elbows and back leg are locked in order to stabilize the body to withstand the impact of the attacker's blade (10.26, 10.27). This block is

10.26

10.27

10.28

10.29

10.30

10.31

executed in the same fashion as tsuba-uke, with the right foot forward, irrespective of the direction from which the attack originates (10.28, 10.29, 10.30, 10.31). The attacks demonstrated here finish with an *ashi-uchi* (leg strike) that can be executed similar to age-uchi (illustrated in pictures 10.30, 10.31).

GEDAN-UKE (LOWER-LEVEL BLOCK)

From chuden kumai, the right foot is shifted slightly, at an oblique angle, to the right or left (depending on the direction of the cut to be deflected). If the attacker utilizes age-uchi or ashi-uchi (from his right side), the right foot shifts position to a left oblique angle, while the kissaki is dropped close to the ground, with the ha toward the left, as the tsuka is shifted to the left. The right arm is fully extended across the front of the body (with the palm facing upward), the left hand is on the pommel (with the palm facing away from the body), and the elbow is positioned at approximately shoulder level. At this point, the sword is at a 45-degree angle, with the kissaki hanging low, aligned with the middle of the opponent's body. The end of the tsuka is approximately at shoulder level (10.32).

The reverse technique is handled in the same manner, although the hands are maneuvered into a reverse position, in order to achieve the opposite, diagonal sword position. The right foot is shifted slightly to the front, at a right oblique angle.

10.32

10.33

10.34

10.35

10.36

Gedan-uke can be used to defend against a horizontal cut to the knees (ashi-uchi: 10.33, 10.34) or age-uchi (rising cut: 10.35, 10.36), but different parts of the sword block the strike. The incoming cut is blocked with the side of the blade (not the ha), if ashi-uchi is utilized, while the tsuba should stop an age-uchi or gyaku age-uchi.

Chapter 11

Ukemi and Shikko-Waza (Falling and Knee-Walking Techniques)

Ukemi, systematic techniques for falling or moving on the ground with a sword, probably arose as a response to the life-or-death situations the samurai inevitably encountered on the battlefield. The ukemi served to protect the samurai sword and enabled the samurai to avoid injury to his person when falling, diving out of harm's way, or clandestinely moving on his knees, utilizing *shikko-waza* in order to execute a stealthy attack. Command of these techniques allowed the samurai to triumph in unexpected, adverse conditions. Be mindful that this aspect of training can be rough on the limbs, so be sure to wear kneepads and/or train on a soft surface to minimize the impact to your body. Also, a novice swordsperson might want to start rolling and falling with a bokken rather than using an iaito or katana because one small mistake might cause a big injury to yourself and to your sword.

MAE UKEMI (FRONT FALL)

When falling to the front, care is taken to avoid falling onto the samurai sword. This could break the sword and cause severe bodily injury, if not death. For *mae ukemi*, stand with the left thumb securing the sheathed blade by the tsuba, and lift the sword (seated in the obi) to the right side of the body until the tsuba is in line with the chin. Bring the right hand across and in front of the left

11.1

11.2

11.3

11.4

arm, keeping the fingers together, with the palm turned toward the front (11.1, 11.2). The feet should be about shoulders' width apart. Dive forward toward the ground, spreading your legs as wide as possible and falling onto the balls of the feet, with the knees locked and buttocks extended up, so the lower part of the body escapes harm (11.3). It is also necessary to turn your head to either side, so that the nose and face aren't injured by the landing. Be sure to keep the arms aligned as described above as you hit the ground (11.4). As you land, continue to cradle the sword with your left hand and take the impact of the fall with the outside of the left forearm, the inside of the right forearm, and the palm of the right hand. Remember that a primary goal of this fall is to minimize the impact of the fall on the samurai sword: cradle the sword as if it were your baby.

YOKO UKEMI (SIDE FALL)

In a manner similar to the front fall, for the side fall, *yoko ukemi*, bring the sheathed sword to the right side of the body, at about chin level, while securing the blade with the left thumb and simultaneously shifting the left foot forward (11.5). Slide the right foot forward (11.6), and bring the right hand across the front of the body to the left side of the chin, with the fingers and thumb slightly bent and close together (11.7).

11.5

11.6

11.7

11.8

11.9

11.10

Continue to slide the right foot forward, keeping the leg straight at the knee, while bending the left knee, and falling back onto the buttocks. On impact, strike the ground with the palm of the right hand, and relax the legs, allowing them to rise (11.8) and then fall downward to the ground. Continue to keep the right leg straight, with the toes pointed forward. During this process, the left knee is bent, and the landing is on the ball of the foot, not on the heel (11.9). Be sure to hold your chin down tightly to your chest, so that the head is prevented from hitting the ground, and the impact to the neck is minimized (11.10). Once again, if you cradle the sword correctly, the back of the scabbard and the end of the handle won't impact the ground directly.

MAE ZEMPO KAITEN (SHEATHED AND UNSHEATHED FRONT ROLL)

SHEATHED

Sheathed *mae zempo kaiten* is performed from shizentai-dachi. Bring the sheathed samurai sword to the right side of the body, with the right hand holding the tsuka and the left hand holding the saya, thereby securing the blade with the thumb. Step forward with the right foot, and, while on the ball of the foot, prepare to execute the rotary roll by bending the left knee deeply (11.11). Keeping the chin tucked to the chest, perform the roll by launching from the legs (11.12). As you roll, make contact

11.11

11.12

11.13

11.14

11.15

11.16

with the ground with the upper part of the right forearm moving all the way up and beyond the right shoulder (11.13, 11.14). Be sure not to direct the kashira into the ground at the beginning of the roll, but do not lower the sword in order to prevent this from happening. If you do, the kojiri will likely hit and break the saya as you finish the roll, because it will be hanging out beyond your side. After the roll has been completed (11.15), reseat the sword deep into the iai obi, as you rise to your feet and stand up (11.16).

UNSHEATHED

From shizentai-dachi, with the blade unsheathed to the side, step forward with the left foot, and bring the saya up with the left hand to about chin level, at the right side of the body (11.17). Step forward with the right foot, and bring the unsheathed blade in front of the body with the right hand, at about a 45-degree angle, with the kissaki hanging downward (11.18, 11.19). While on the ball of the foot, bend the left knee deeply, keeping the saya secured near the right shoulder, and bend the chin to the chest, as you execute the roll (11.20). The body first makes contact with the ground at

11.17

11.18

11.19

11.20

11.21

11.22

11.23

approximately the upper forearm, with the sword's kissaki staying to the left side of the body during the roll (11.21). In a manner similar to the sheathed method, make contact with the ground above the forearm and beyond the right shoulder (11.22). As you stand up at the completion of the roll, the sword is directed straight to the front, and the saya is seated back into the iai obi (11.23).

SHIKKO-WAZA (KNEE-WALKING TECHNIQUE)

Starting in seiza, with the left hand on the saya, securing the blade with the left thumb, and the right hand on the tsuka, rise onto the balls of both feet, and onto the left knee. The right knee is up, and the buttocks are seated on the heels of both feet, which is a position called *han-sankyo* (11.24). This position permits easy movement on the knees by allowing one to drop the elevated front knee, turn, and reposition the feet, keeping them close to one another, with the knee that was in the back assuming an upright position to the front. In this particular example, the right knee drops to the ground (11.25), and you then swivel clockwise on that knee, bringing the left knee forward and off the ground to the upright position, pointing to the front. The feet slide together to the left, and the buttocks rest on top of the heels just before executing another

11.24

11.25

11.26

11.27

11.28

movement to the front (11.26). To continue forward from this position, drop the left knee to the ground (11.27), and swivel counter-clockwise, bringing the right knee forward and off the ground to the upright position, pointing to the front. The feet slide together to the right, and the buttocks rest on top of the heels again (11.28).

Twisting to the left and right with the upper torso, after dropping onto the knees in this manner, permits rapid and smooth movement forward. While twisting the upper body, be careful not to direct the tsuka toward the rear, because you must always be able to execute a draw to the front when moving on the knees in a forward direction. In addition, always position yourself on the balls of both feet when moving on the knees. This allows you to draw while on your knees, and to stand at any time.

Ken-Jutsu Solo Training

Whether you are unable to attend a formal class or simply wish to practice on your own, solo ken-jutsu training is easy to do.

If the muscles of your body are well conditioned, begin by taking a sub-urito, poised for ken-jutsu training. (If you do not consider yourself to be in good shape, I advise starting with a bokken and beginning by assuming shizentai-dachi.) Grip the tsuka (utilizing te-moto) and position the body into each kumai, with the objective of transitioning the hands and feet smoothly and without hesitation. Return back to shizentai-dachi and practice moving across the floor using tsugi-ashi, with the right arm hanging relaxed and the sword at the side of the body. When you are comfortable, practice suburi (cutting) from a stationary position, deepening the posture by bending the knees and utilizing the shoulders for speed and power. Follow by coordinating tsugi-ashi with each cut, so the arms and posture move in tandem with each other. Slowly accelerate the momentum of the techniques as they become increasingly smooth and effortless.

I firmly believe that the *quantity* of techniques that one can execute is secondary to the *quality* with which they are executed. Practice your techniques repetitively and exhaustively until your body has been conditioned to replicate movements "on demand," with very little thought. Once this has been achieved, try combining a variety of different cuts in sequence, with the objective of transitioning from one to the next in a fluid manner. Beware lest you forget to slide with each cut, for your power will be compromised greatly without this motion. Whether you are sliding forward or backward, movement unequivocally improves the technique.

Chapter 12

Iai-Jutsu

Like the gunslingers of America's Wild West, samurai engaging in battle depended on the speed and accuracy of their draw to determine their fate: any hesitation or small mistake in technique could result in death. And just as the gun posed a significant hazard to its user, the blade was a threat to its bearer. It was therefore imperative that the samurai strictly adhere to the intricate and elaborate techniques of safely drawing and sheathing the samurai sword taught in the martial art of iai-jutsu. In addition, it was of paramount importance that the swordsman's eyes be focused on his environment in order to react to approaching evil, even while drawing or sheathing. Because of this, techniques of drawing and sheathing the samurai sword require a heightened sense of touch, rather than reliance upon the sense of sight.

Clearly, a high level of skill was required in order to master drawing and sheathing this simple looking, yet complex weapon. The three most important elements of iai-jutsu—nuki-dashi (drawing), chiburi (deblooding) and noto (sheathing)—are explored below.

NUKI-DASHI (DRAWING)

The following exercises start from *musubi-dachi*, a posture with the heels in close proximity to one another and the feet

12.1

directed in opposite, oblique angles in a V formation (12.1). It should be understood that there are many postures from which to commence and conclude samurai sword techniques; however, the standing katas, or forms, unique to Fukasa-Ryu iai-jutsu begin from this position. And so it is in musubi-dachi that we will start applying our sense of touch during the sword-drawing process.

It is important to be mindful of two major parts of the samurai sword during the drawing process: the saya and the ha. As the saya is withdrawn from the sword, care must be exercised to avoid cutting the inside of the saya. This is accomplished by using the left hand to push the saya lightly against the mune as the blade is unsheathed. Please take notice of my choice of words here: "unsheathe" and "withdraw" the saya from the blade—the sword is unsheathed rather than "drawn" from the scabbard, which implies that the majority of the motion is to pull back on the Saya. The blade will be exposed as it is drawn forward slightly. Subsequent to any and all draws, the saya should be immediately returned to the same location, the left hip, and positioned in the same upright direction, which historically would have allowed the samurai to be confident that he could sheathe his blade quickly at any time. Having to ascertain the position of the saya during battle could be a dangerous thing!

NUKI-DASHI AGE (RISING OBLIQUE DRAW)

From musubi-dachi (12.2), move the sheathed sword forward far enough that the left elbow can rest on the saya (12.3). Turn the left hand to the left, so that the ha (still sheathed) is facing downward, to the left, at an oblique angle (12.4). Follow by sliding the tip of the thumb below the tsuba, which was preventing the blade from inadvertently unsheathing. Push the tsuba forward with the thumb, exposing the habaki

12.2

12.3

12.4

12.5

12.6

12.7

from the koiguchi, to loosen the sword from its saya (12.5). Place the back of the right open hand onto the tsuka (12.6) and prepare to grip the handle correctly by feel, rather than by taking your attention away from your target. Then, slide the right hand down the tsuka and grab it at the tsuba by inverting the wrist (12.7). Keeping the ha in the same direction, slide the right foot forward at a right, oblique angle, assuming zenkutsu-dachi, with the front knee bent and the back leg straightened and locked at the knee. The body is now "rooted" for drawing power. Simultaneously, shift the seated sword, as a single unit, forward slightly (12.8). Finally, draw, by pulling back on the saya and returning it to its original upward-facing position seated in the sword obi. Unsheathe the blade (12.9), and then guide the sword in a diagonal motion to rise from the left to the right. At the conclusion of the draw, the swordsman's arm is fully extended to the right side of the front of the body, with the ha pointed upward at a

12.8

12.9

12.10

12.11

45-degree angle. The right arm is held slightly higher than shoulder level, and the kissaki hangs suspended in line with the chin or neck area (rendering the entire length of the sword at an oblique angle, pointed upward to the right) (12.10). Finishing in this position keeps an attacker at bay, with the swordsman protected against a linear attack from the front.

Nuki-Dashi Tate (Vertical Draw)

From musubi-dachi, slide the left foot forward slightly, bending the back, right knee deeply, assuming *neko-ashi-dachi,* or "cat stance." The left foot is flat, rather than poised on the ball of the foot. Lift the sheathed blade vertically with the left hand, so the tsuba is around the same height as the chin. The left elbow and forearm should be flat against the back of the saya, at the upper-left side of the body (12.11). At this point, the ha remains in a vertical, upward position (12.12), just as it was seated in the drawer's belt. With eyes still focused on the target, the back of the open, right hand is placed on the topside of the tsuka, after the

12.12

12.13

12.14

12.15

thumb has pushed upward on the tsuba, removing the habaki from the saya (12.13, 12.14). The thumb continues to exert force on the bottom of the tsuba, keeping it clear slightly from the koiguchi, until you begin to unsheathe the blade. Next, slide the right hand down to the tsuba and turn it over, in order to grab the tsuka properly (12.15, 12.16). Draw the sword by simultaneously deepening the posture, as the blade is unsheathed through pulling downward on the saya (12.17). Return the saya to its original

12.16

12.17

12.18

position in the obi. This unsheathing provides a particularly smooth transition into a shomen-uchi (head cut). To execute this, bring the tsuka directly overhead with the right hand (12.18), and grasp the end of the tsuka with the left hand, if a two-handed shomen-uchi to the front is desired.

Nuki-Dashi Tomoe (Horizontal Stomach Draw)

This draw is executed using the same foot and hand movements as nuki-dashi age. The ha is turned to the left prior to unsheathing, however, and will be drawn horizontally at stomach–level, with the blade parallel to the ground at all times (12.19–12.25). Since the objective of the move is to cut the entire width of the body, the draw ends with the tsuka positioned at stomach height, to the front, right side of the drawer's body, with the kissaki pointing straight ahead (12.26). The sword can be quickly maneuvered to one's center for protection, as the kissaki would not travel far beyond the side of the enemy's body (12.27).

12.19

Nuki-Dashi Ushiro (Rear Draw)

In musubi-dachi, the left hand rotates the sheathed blade 180 degrees to the left, with the ha pointing in the direction of the ground (12.28). The left thumb pushes the tsuba forward, in preparation for the draw (12.29). The right, open hand slides down the underside of the tsuka as the knees are gradually bent (12.30, 12.31). Using this reverse grip, the

12.20

12.21

12.22

12.23

12.24

12.25

12.26

12.27

12.28

12.29

12.30

12.31

12.32

12.33

12.34

12.35

samurai sword is drawn, pulling the tsuka upward so that the tsuba stops above the level of the eyes, with the blade vertical in front of the body (12.32, 12.33). Return the saya to its original, pre-drawing position. This unsheathing allows one to transition easily into ushiro-tsuki (rear thrust). To execute this, the left hand should grasp the end of the tsuka, with the pinky finger on the kashira, and the palm turned to the left. The mune is then stabilized against the bottom of the right forearm, by bending at the right wrist (12.34). The swordsman looks to the rear, at the right side of his or her body, slides the right foot back into zenkutsu-dachi (locked knee posture), and the kissaki is then thrust straight to the rear by movement of

12.36

the right elbow and left (pushing) hand (12.35, 12.36). In battlefield situations, the sword would need to be extricated from the opponent's body subsequent to the thrust.

Nuki-Dashi Seiza (Seated Draw)

Nuki-dashi age (12.37–12.39), tate (12.40, 12.41), tomoe (12.42, 12.43) and ushiro (12.44–12.49) can all be executed from seiza, a seated position on your knees with your feet crossed one atop the other, behind you, and your backside resting comfortably on your heels. Drawing from seiza is done in a manner similar to the standing methods; the only minor modification made in each case is in the movement of the legs. Instead of shifting the right foot forward just prior to unsheathing the blade, the swordsman shifts onto the left knee. This will provide adequate momentum for the draw. In the case of nuki-dashi ushiro from seiza, a similar movement onto the left knee is used. This movement is executed, however, simultaneously with the removal of the blade from its scabbard.

CHIBURI (DEBLOODING)

The chiburi was a necessary procedure performed by the samurai after the samurai sword had been extricated from the flesh of an opponent, just prior to being resheathed in its saya. Chiburi was not a method of wiping the blade completely free of blood. It was a way of whisking or flicking the greater portion of blood (or

12.37

12.38

12.39

12.40

12.41

12.42

12.43

12.44

12.45

12.46

12.47

12.48

12.49

other residues) off the blade, and to the end of the blade, where it could easily be discarded before the blade was sheathed in its scabbard. Any residue, but especially sticky blood, could cause a sluggish draw or, even worse, prevent a swordsman from withdrawing his saya—a circumstance that could very well result in death. Many methods evolved to safeguard against these difficulties, including the following deblooding techniques utilized in Fukasa-Ryu iai-jutsu.

CHIBURI ICHI-WAZA (DEBLOODING TECHNIQUE #1)

From migi zenkutsu-dachi (the back, left leg locked at the knee), the samurai sword is held at the front, right side of the body next to the right leg (12.50), hanging relaxed in the right hand with the ha and kissaki pointed downward, close to the ground. With a hard stomp of the heel of the right foot, the right wrist is forcefully turned to

12.50

12.51

the left, repositioning the kissaki, which hangs close to the ground, with the ha facing diagonally downward, directly in line with the swordsman's center (12.51). The length of the sword should appear to be protecting the front of the swordsman's body in a manner similar to the final position of nuki-dashi age, but here the sword is positioned close to the ground.

CHIBURI NI-WAZA (DEBLOODING TECHNIQUE #2)

In the same posture as chiburi ichi-waza, the samurai sword is now held by the right hand in a vertical position, with the tsuba at approximately chin level, and the elbow bent against the side of the body (12.52, 12.53). With the ha facing forward, the sword is swung counterclockwise overhead, circling from right to left (12.54), and then diagonally downward (12.55), from left to right, in front of the body. This is one fluid movement, executed with a relaxed wrist, and finishing with the right arm, elbow locked, fully extended just beyond the right leg (12.56).

12.52

12.53

12.54

12.55

12.56

CHIBURI SEIZA
(SEATED DEBLOODING TECHNIQUE)

Chiburi ichi-waza is the only method of deblooding that is executed from the kneeling position. It commences with the right knee up (12.57), followed by a movement of the knee to the right, shifting off the sole of the foot onto its right side, as the right wrist is snapped (turning left) (12.58, 12.59).

12.57

12.58

12.59

NOTO (SHEATHING)

While the chiburi entails aggressively ridding the blade of residue by swinging the blade, snapping the wrist, and even hitting the tsuka firmly with the wrist in some cases, the noto includes wiping the remnants of residue from the hi (blood groove) with the fingers and thumb. There are two basic methods of noto that Fukasa-Ryu iai-jutsu employs: the stomach (horizontal) and vertical sheathings.

NOTO TOMOE (*HORIZONTAL STOMACH SHEATHING*)

After the chiburi (in migi zenkutsu-dachi), the saya is pulled forward from the iai obi, far enough so that the left elbow is straightened. The saya is straight out from the obi, parallel to the ground (12.60, 12.61). Next, the saya is turned to the left, so the left palm faces upward (12.62). The right hand then brings the mune, at the beginning of the monouchi, approximately three-quarters of the length toward the end of the blade, to the koiguchi. Grasp the blade by its hi with the thumb and index finger of the left hand, being careful not to let go of the saya and not to touch the ha (12.63, 12.64, 12.65). At this point, the blade and saya are perpendicular, with the horizontal blade at stomach level, in front. Grip the hi with the left hand, as the right hand pulls the tsuka directly to the right, sliding the sword through the fingers (12.66), causing any residue to fall off the blade before it is sheathed. When the end of the hi is sensed by

12.60

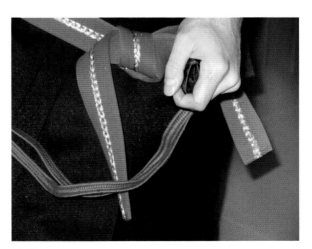

12.61

12.62

12.63

12.64

12.65

12.66

12.67

the fingers, with eyes always focused on the opponent and environment, ready for attack, slowly retract the saya into the iai obi, allowing the kissaki to safely slide into the koiguchi (12.67, 12.68, 12.69, 12.70). The tsuka and saya are immediately turned upward (so the ha is in an upward direction), once they are positioned straight to the front, on the left side of the body (12.71). The saya then slides upward to the tsuba (12.72, 12.73), sheathing the sword, and the left thumb locks the sword into place by latching onto the top of the tsuba (12.74). The right hand then releases the tsuka, and positions its palm onto the kashira, with fingers together, pointing to the left (12.75). Last, the left foot slides halfway forward to the swordsman's center, and the right foot slides back to meet it halfway, in musubi-dachi. The back is then straightened, and the chest moves forward as the sword is once again seated back into its iai obi (12.76, 12.77).

12.68

12.69

12.70

12.71

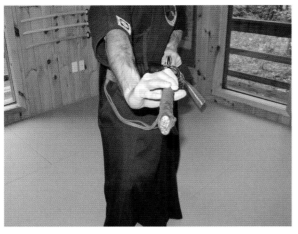

12.72

12.73

12.74

12.75

12.76

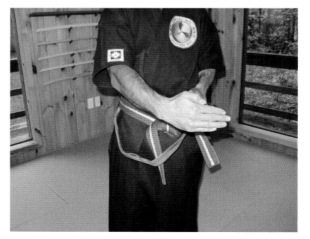

12.77

NOTO TATE (VERTICAL SHEATHING)

From chiburi, the saya is once again brought forward from the iai obi, as in noto tomoe (12.78). The right foot follows by sliding forward slightly, as the sword is turned to a vertical position and is moved by the right hand across the front of the body to the left side. The kissaki faces to the rear at an oblique angle, and the ha faces the swordsman's front, with the tsuka held near the leg region. The hi is once again gripped by the left thumb and index finger, and the bottom of the mune (mune-machi, just above the habaki) lies just below the bottom of the koiguchi (12.79, 12.80, 12.81). (Note: The mune at all times rests flat across the koiguchi.) The right knee bends slowly, as the tsuka is simultaneously drawn downward at an oblique angle (12.82). At the same time, the saya slides back and up toward the blade's kissaki (12.83). When the end of the hi is sensed, the tsuka is lifted, and the saya is lowered

12.78

12.79

12.80

12.81

12.82

12.83

12.84

12.85

12.86

12.87

12.88

gradually, until the kissaki slips into the saya, straightening both blade and scabbard to the front (12.84). (They are still at the left side of the swordsman's body.) At this point, the left hand sheaths the blade and locks it by clipping the tsuba with the left thumb (12.85). With the palm open, the right hand then moves to the end of the tsuka, in a manner similar to noto tomoe (12.86). The left foot slides forward halfway to the swordsman's center, and the right foot slides back, both feet meeting in musubi-dachi. The back is then straightened, and the chest moves forward, as the blade is once again seated in its original position in the iai obi (12.87, 12.88).

Noto Seiza (Seated Sheathing)

In seiza, noto tomoe (12.89–12.92) and noto tate (12.93–12.99) are both executed in the same manner as when standing. They are conducted, however, with the right knee up, rather than the right foot forward. In addition, the hakama (skirt) is "popped" or pushed under the knee (12.91), with the right hand, after the samurai sword has been properly seated in its iai obi. This procedure is followed in order to allow the swordsman to draw again without getting his or her legs caught in the hakama. The swordsman then drops to seiza (12.92).

12.89

12.90

12.91

12.92

12.93

12.94

12.95

12.96

12.97

12.98

(Note: always be sure to rise to the ball of the back foot whenever lifting a knee. This permits you to stand and root yourself for a balanced technique. In addition, the sword is always held locked in the left hand, with the thumb on the tsuba, while "popping" the hakama under the leg, regardless of which knee is being lowered to the ground. Only the right hand is to be used to manipulate the hakama. It is also important to "pop" the hakama just prior to kneeling on either knee, in order to avoid stumbling when rising.)

12.99

Iai-Jutsu Solo Training

As with ken-jutsu, you can practice iai-jutsu outside of a formal classroom situation. Following training in ken-jutsu with iai-jutsu training can work well for those practicing on their own, as it can provide some welcome relief from the stress placed on the shoulders, arms, and legs by the ken-jutsu techniques.

Begin your practice by standing relaxed, your feet about a shoulders' width apart, with a seated iaito affixed to your left side. Let the right arm hang relaxed at the right side of the body, and secure the blade by holding the saya with the left hand around the area of the kurigata, with the thumb locked on the tsuba. Close your eyes and take a few deep breaths. Once your body feels at ease and your mind is clear of all thoughts, open your eyes and begin following a drawing sequence.

If you are an absolute beginner, I suggest starting with nuki-dashi age, the most frequently used and easiest sword-draw to learn. Follow each aspect of the draw in its proper sequence, and be mindful of your posture. Proceed with the subtle manipulations of the hands that affect the positioning of the sword and its scabbard. Attentiveness to these fine details will prevent the sword from bending and the saya from being damaged or possibly breaking.

Once the nuki-dashi age becomes less laborious, add a chiburi and noto technique. Sheathe the blade slowly, utilizing the sense of touch rather than the eyes to guide the kissaki into the koiguchi. Try to resist the urge to watch your hands, keeping your eyes focused toward the front, while visualizing the blade entering the scabbard. With persistence, patience, and time, what might have once been a daunting cerebral and physical task will become automatic and natural.

Chapter 13

Katas (Standing Forms)

Katas, an important legacy left by masters of the Asian martial arts, are tutorials that model the proper way to execute techniques in sequence. In some cases, katas are the only "living," remnants of the original teachings that represent the true wisdom and vision of the founders of the martial arts. A kata that is pure, that hasn't been modified, can be likened to a primary text that directly reflects the author's perspective, rather than the interpretation of a translator, who creates a biased, secondary text.

In iai-jutsu and ken-jutsu, katas were probably formulated by samurai who had time to reflect upon their battle experiences. A swordsman might have thought carefully about an individual bout or series of bouts and contemplated how he had thwarted the attacks successfully. By modeling these techniques in the form of a kata, the swordsman could teach his young apprentice (usually a son) how to perform them effectively. Katas appeared at a later stage of a martial art's development and were probably developed during a "down time," a time of peace when a swordsman could contemplate the most efficacious execution of technique.

Katas serve many functions, some of which might not be readily evident to a novice martial arts practitioner. The kata aspect of samurai sword training can have a positive effect on the body by calming the mind while simultaneously exercising the muscles. I believe that the continuous repetition of strings of techniques, via the practice of these forms, eventually conditions the body to automatically move and respond to attacks correctly, following the wisdom of the kata. The complexity of the techniques of the Fukasa-Ryu kata and the rigorousness by which one practices these techniques transform both the mind and the body. I view kata as "meditation through movement," because complete focus is required while executing kata with the weapon. A student must clear the mind, relax, and yield only to the "storyline" of the kata, a prefabricated sequence of techniques that are efficient responses to "visualized" impending attacks. The degree to which one immerses oneself cognitively in the kata, coupled with the physical energy expended, usually determines the depth of one's meditation during kata practice.

On a physical, muscular level, kata practice builds strength and endurance and can burn calories like any comparably sustained, rigorous exercise. As it pertains to sword use, regular kata practice can help to expedite draws, add power and speed to cuts, increase endurance, and serve as extra training time. Repetitive drawing and cutting, through the course of kata practice, strengthens the shoulders, triceps, and grip, toning the upper portion of the body. Maximum physical benefit can be achieved by practicing katas rigorously, in succession, with pauses between forms being kept to a minimum, thus challenging the heart and receiving the many benefits of aerobic exercise.

The katas of Fukasa-Ryu iai-jutsu, designed by me, represent years of contemplation of the techniques of the samurai sword with reference to economy of motion, or efficient transition from one technique to the next, and pragmatism, or combat effectiveness. Also incorporated into Fukasa-Ryu iai-jutsu are the esoteric katas that I've had the honor to learn and practice during the past thirty years as a student of the martial arts. Kata practice is the most effective way to train in the samurai sword if you do not have a partner. It does not, however, replace bogyo-waza (defensive) training against an opponent.

FUKASA-RYU IAI-JUTSU KISO KATA: STANDING FORMS

KATA MAE (FRONT FORM)

From musubi-dachi, perform nuki-dashi age (13.1). Bring the left foot forward to return to musubi-dachi, while circling the blade overhead to grip the tsuka with the left hand (13.2, 13.3). Execute shomen-uchi, while sliding the right foot forward into migi zenkutsu-dachi (13.4). Finish by employing chiburi ichi-waza, followed by noto tate. Step back with the right foot, then the left foot, and finally the right foot

13.1

13.2

13.3

13.4

13.5

once again, ending in musubi-dachi, with the feet together.

Kata Migi (Right Form)

From musubi-dachi, glance to the right (13.5) then look straight ahead, shift the whole sheathed sword forward from the obi and slide the left foot forward slightly, while placing the back of the right hand on the tsuka (13.6). Turn over the right hand at the tsuba, grab the tsuka, and retract the sword while sliding the right foot forward beside the left foot (13.7).

13.6

13.7

13.8

13.9

13.10

13.11

13.12

Turn to the right and slide the right foot to the right (13.8), while performing a pommel strike (kashira-uchi) to the hara by bringing the tsuka and saya forward and then reseating them into the obi (13.9, 13.10). Next, tap the left leg with the right foot, while twisting the blade into position for nuki-dachi age (13.11). Perform nuki-dashi age in this direction, after landing in migi zenkutsu-dachi, with the right arm and sword extended (13.12, 13.13). Then, slide the back, left foot forward next to the right foot. Prepare the sword for a kubi-uchi, by turning the right wrist upward, so the sword is positioned at a 45-degree angle, with the tsuka positioned above the right side of the head. Grab the bottom of the tsuka with the left hand (13.14, 13.15) and execute kubi-uchi, while sliding the right foot forward into migi zenkutsu-dachi (13.16). Last, look to the left (the direction you faced at the beginning of this kata) (13.17), and slide the right foot in that direction by pivoting on the left foot (assuming migi

13.13

13.14

13.15

13.16

13.17

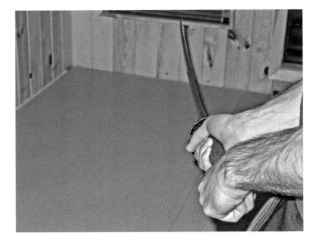

13.18

13.19

13.20

13.21

13.22

zenkutsu-dachi, once again). At the same time, bring the sword to the right side, cocking it at about stomach level (13.18), and sweep it (13.19) horizontally across to the left, at stomach level, parallel to the ground—thus "clearing" the front of the body (13.20) and transitioning into a shomen-uchi (13.21, 13.22). Perform chiburi ichiwaza and noto tate. To finish, slide one step across to the left with the left foot, and follow by sliding one step back with the right foot. You are now situated at your *enbusen* (beginning point).

KATA HIDARI (LEFT FORM)

In musubi-dachi, make contact with the upper part of the tsuka with the back of the right hand (13.23), preparing to grab it, and slide the right hand slowly downward toward the tsuba, while bending gradually at the knees. Simultaneously twist the ha

13.23

toward the left with the left wrist (until the ha is pointed to the left), and stealthily turn the head toward the left. After feeling the tsuba, grab the tsuka with the right hand, and perform nuki-dashi by pulling the tsuka from its saya, upward in

13.24

13.25

a 45-degree angle to the right, to the front of the body (13.24). Spin the blade overhead in a clockwise direction, and slide the right foot out to the left, while performing a one-handed kubi-uchi (which is executed in the same way as kubi-uchi, but with the right hand alone) (13.25, 13.26, 13.27). Next, bring the left foot forward to the right, while cocking the blade overhead, grabbing the sword with the left hand as well (13.28). Execute shomen-uchi by sliding the right foot forward into migi zenkutsu-dachi (13.29). Last, look to the original front (right), slide the right foot to the right and pivot on the left foot, assuming migi zenkutsu-dachi (13.30). Simultaneously, shift the sword into the gyaku-no kumai position, and execute gyaku age-uchi (13.31). Perform chiburi ichi-waza and noto tate. Return to the enbusen by sliding the right leg one foot to the right, then sliding the left foot to the rear.

13.26

13.27

13.28

13.29

13.30

13.31

13.32

13.33

KATA USHIRO (REAR FORM)

From musubi-dachi, slide the left foot forward slightly and execute nuki-dashi tate (13.32). Still facing forward, holding the tsuka, drop the right hand to chest level, and bring the mune (unsharpened part of the blade) at the beginning of the monouchi to the palm of the open, left hand (13.33). Next, turn right 180 degrees to the rear, and slide the right foot into migi zenkutsu-dachi (13.34, 13.35) while performing a supported neck-level, horizontal cut (*yokumen sasse-uchi*) (13.36, 13.37). Remove the left hand from the mune, and bring the blade clockwise around the body and overhead with the right hand. With the left hand, finish by grabbing the end of the tsuka at the right side of the head and executing kubi-uchi in place (13.38, 13.39, 13.40, 13.41). Perform chiburi ichi-waza and noto tate. Return to the original direction, into the enbusen, by turning 180 degrees to the right with a tight about-face (13.42, 13.43).

13.34

13.35

13.36

13.37

13.38

13.39

13.40

13.41

13.42

13.43

KATA MAE, USHIRO NUKI-UCHI (FRONT, REAR JUMP-CUT FORM)

From musubi-dachi, perform nuki-dashi tomoe to the front (13.44). Bring the left foot forward to the right foot while circling the sword overhead (13.45, 13.46), and perform shomen-uchi to the front, as the right foot slides forward into migi zenkutsu-dachi (13.47). In one quick movement, while jumping, circle the sword counterclockwise in the left direction to the rear, at stomach height.

13.44

13.45

13.46

13.47

13.48

13.49

While suspended in the air, bring the blade overhead to perform nuki-uchi (13.48, 13.49, 13.50). Finish the vertical, downward cut as you land lightly on the left knee and the ball of the left foot (with the right knee off the ground), with the blade extending forward, parallel to the ground, as in chuden kumai (13.51). The jump has been done in place, with each foot assuming the other's position at the finish. The kata concludes by rising off the left knee into migi zenkutsu-dachi and performing chiburi ichi-waza and noto tate. A 180-degree spin to the right, similar to kata ushiro, is executed, and then followed by a right, left, then right step to the rear, ending at the enbusen.

KATA KAZE KIRU (WHIRLWIND FORM)

From musubi-dachi, execute nuki-dashi tate, and grab the bottom of the tsuka with the left hand (13.52). Perform shomen-uchi from the draw by sliding the right foot forward into migi zenkutsu-dachi after the grab (13.53). Turn 180 degrees to the left rear by pivoting

13.50

13.51

13.52

13.53

13.54

13.55

13.56

13.57

13.58

on the left foot (13.54) and sliding the right foot (13.55), and perform shomen-uchi by bringing the sword straight over to the rear, assuming migi zenkutsu-dachi (13.56). Next, slide the right foot to the right (13.57), toward the original frontal position, into a posture called *keba dachi* ("horse stance"), assuming a deep posture. Perform kashira-uchi by thrusting the end of the tsuka to the right, using the ha upward (13.58). The sword is parallel to the ground. Look and spin to the left (original rear), sliding the right foot, while pivoting on

13.59

13.60

13.61

13.62

the left, to perform a one-handed clearing motion (a swing of the blade to clear an area of any obstacles), with the ha horizontal, directed to the left, at neck level (13.59, 13.60). Continue the movement to the left by sliding the right foot back to the original forward position, while simultaneously bringing the blade clockwise around (13.61, 13.62) and overhead, for a two-handed shomen-uchi (13.63, 13.64, 13.65). Conclude by performing chiburi ichi-waza and noto tate.

13.63

13.64

13.65

13.66

13.67

KATA USHIRO NUKI-UCHI
(REAR JUMP-CUT FORM)

From musubi-dachi, slide the left foot slightly forward for nuki-dashi tate (13.66). Crouch deeply into the stance in preparation for the jump (13.67), and then jump in place, spinning 180 degrees to the left, as the draw is executed by bringing the blade overhead (13.68) and then downward into a shomen-uchi. Land lightly on the left knee and the ball of the left foot (13.69). Finish by standing and performing chiburi ichiwaza and noto tate. Move to face in the original direction by turning 180 degrees to the right, as in kata mae, ushiro nuki-uchi.

13.69

13.68

KATA MIGI, HIDARI, MAE (RIGHT, LEFT, FRONT FORM)

In musubi-dachi, scan to your right and left periphery by turning your head from right (13.70) to left (13.71). When the eyes and head are positioned to the left, shift the left foot forward slightly and draw the sword, executing nuki-dashi tate (13.72, 13.73). Once the blade is unsheathed overhead, grasp the bottom of the tsuka with the left hand (13.74) for a shomen-uchi to the right, while sliding the right foot to the right, into migi zenkutsu-dachi (13.75). Next, follow with an immediate shomen-uchi to the rear, by sliding the right foot to the left,

13.71

13.70

13.72

13.73

13.74

13.75

13.76

turning 180 degrees (13.76, 13.77, 13.78). This cut is accomplished by raising the blade directly from chuden kumai (the finishing position of the first shomen-uchi), above the head, and then bringing it down (rather than using a circular, clearing motion). Next, shift the right foot 90 degrees to the right, original, front position (into migi zenkutsu-dachi) and perform tomoe sasse-uchi (supported stomach-level cut) (13.79, 13.80, 13.81). Slide the left foot forward into hidari zenkutsu-dachi, while rotating the ha downward, and positioning the

13.77

13.78

13.79

13.80

13.81

13.82

13.83

13.84

13.85

13.86

sword at the level of the hara (13.82). The hands are kept in the same location on the sword, with the right hand positioned at the right hip, gripping the tsuka, and the left hand on top of the mune. Execute mae-tsuki (front thrust) with the palm of the left hand on the mune, fingers positioned close together, pointed to the right. Keep the blade straight, as the right hand, gripping the tsuka, thrusts the blade forward (similar to the way in which a pool cue is manipulated, using a forward, then backward, motion) (13.83, 13.84). Finish by sliding the right foot one more step forward into migi zenkutsu-dachi, while parrying (swinging) the blade overhead with the right hand, for a one-handed kubi-uchi (13.85, 13.86, 13.87). Perform chiburi ichi-waza and noto tate. Slide back the right, left, right, then left foot, to the enbusen (ending in musubi-dachi).

KATA SHIKAZE (FOUR WINDS FORM)

From musubi-dachi, shift the left foot and sword forward slightly, and glance to the left, while turning the ha to the left and placing the

13.87

13.88

back of the right hand onto the tsuka (13.88). Turn 270 degrees to the right and perform nuki-dashi tomoe (13.89, 13.90, 13.91). The swordsman now faces to the left of the original, front direction. Tap the left leg with the right foot and shift forward slightly, utilizing the "following foot" method, tsugi-ashi. Parry the blade counterclockwise to the front and overhead into shomen-uchi (13.92, 13.93). Follow by bringing the blade perpendicular to the front by bending the left hand at the wrist, and releasing the grip with the right hand, rotating the right hand over into a reverse position atop the tsuka. Position the mune tightly against the bottom of the right forearm, preparing to execute ushiro-tsuki (rear thrust) to the right (13.94). Turn the upper torso to the left, lock the back knee, step back with the right foot, and thrust the sword to the rear (13.95). Release the grip of the tsuka with the right hand, and slide it to the rear, over the tsuba, and onto the mune. The right hand is now positioned vertically on the mune, with fingertips held together, three-

13.89

13.90

13.91

13.92

13.93

13.94

13.95

quarters of the way to the beginning of the monouchi (13.96). Slide the right foot forward (to the original, rear direction) and execute age sasse-uchi (supported, upward vertical cut), first downward (13.97) and then in an ascending motion (13.98), cutting vertically up the center of your imagined opponent's body (13.99). Continue the cutting motion as you turn 180 degrees to the left, and again slide the right foot. Conclude the supported cut at the level of the hara, lowering the blade (13.100) as it cuts vertically. Turn the right

13.96

13.97

13.98

13.99

hand, which is still on the mune, to the left (with fingers pointed in that direction), and execute mae-tsuki (13.101, 13.102) with the left hand on the tsuka, as in kata migi, hidari, mae. Slide the right, open hand back up the mune and over the tsuba, and grip the tsuka on the topside, utilizing a reverse grip (13.103, 13.104). Then release the tsuka with the left hand, slide the right foot out to the right (13.105), and perform a double-figure-eight, reverse-grip cut, in that direction (13.106, 13.107, 13.108, 13.109). Finish the cut by

13.100

13.101

13.102

13.103

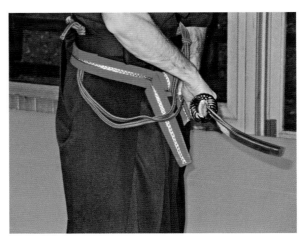

13.104

13.105

13.106

bringing the mune directly to the saya (13.110, 13.111), in order to prepare for noto tate. There is no need for another chiburi; it is part of the double-figure-eight cut. Subsequent to the noto, shift 90 degrees to the left (the original forward direction) by leading with the left foot, redirecting into musubi-dachi toward the left.

13.107

13.108

13.109

13.110

13.111

Chapter 14

Seiza Katas (Kneeling Forms)

In addition to the standing position, sword techniques are also practiced from the seated position, and on the knees, as well. At a time of rest, when kneeling comfortably to eat, mindfully meditating, or just relaxing, a samurai had his sword close by his side. He had to be well trained in how to respond to an attack from this position. Hence, the contemporary swordsperson should develop the same sword skills. You will find that these kneeling forms are challenging, but through practice—as you rise and fall onto your knees while drawing, cutting, and sheathing the samurai sword—they build the muscles of the legs and increase overall physical endurance. This kind of practice requires soft ground, a matted area, or use of kneepads to soften the impact to the knees.

FUKASA-RYU IAI-JUTSU KISO: KNEELING FORMS

KATA MAE (FRONT FORM)

From seiza, perform nuki-dashi age (14.1). Parry the blade overhead (14.2), and follow with shomen-uchi, to the front (14.3). Finish by executing chiburi and noto tate from the knee. (Note: All katas from seiza utilize the same vertical sheathing technique.)

14.1

14.2

14.3

KATA MIGI (RIGHT FORM)

From seiza, look quickly to the right (14.4), then turn the head back to the front, while preparing for a modified nuki-dashi tomoe. Draw the sword by turning the ha to the horizontal position, facing to the left (14.5), and withdrawing the blade from its scabbard. As the blade is withdrawn, rise up from the right knee (onto the left knee) and turn 90 degrees to the right (14.6). Simultaneously, with fingers pointed upward, place the left hand on the mune (14.7), preparing for tomoe sasse-uchi from the kneeling position. Execute a horizontal, supported cut (14.8), and then follow with a shomen-uchi, by circling the blade overhead (14.9, 14.10), in the same "knee up"

14.4

14.5

14.6

14.7

14.8

14.9

position. Execute chiburi and noto tate from the knee, "pop" the right side of the hakama, and fall, repositioning the body to the original position, facing front, and ending in seiza.

KATA HIDARI, MAE (LEFT, FRONT FORM)

From seiza, look quickly to the left (14.11), and then back to the front, as if focusing straight ahead, with the intention of drawing to the front. At the same time, rotate the ha downward 180 degrees with the left hand, and place the back of the right, open hand on the

14.10

14.11

14.12

14.13

14.14

14.15

tsuka (14.12). Draw the sword in a manner similar to nuki-dashi ushiro from seiza, but use a regular (not reverse) grip, with the right hand withdrawing the blade without bringing the saya forward. This is done while lifting the right knee, followed by spinning on the left knee, 90 degrees in the left direction (14.13, 14.14). As in the illustration, the blade is located at the right side, at hip level, in line with the leg, and parallel to the ground, with the kissaki pointed to the front (14.15). Mae-tsuki (front thrust) is carried out from this

14.16

14.17

14.18

14.19

posture by thrusting the blade forward with the right hand (14.16) and then bringing it back to the hip (14.17). Next, a two-handed kubi-uchi is quickly executed by parrying the blade around the front and overhead (14.18, 14.19, 14.20), followed by a repositioning of the posture, shifting the right foot 90 degrees into the original, frontal direction (14.21). The tsuka is moved directly overhead (without a parrying motion) (14.22) in preparation for a quick shomen-uchi to the front (14.23). After the shomen-uchi has been executed,

14.20

14.21

14.22

14.23

14.24

14.25

chiburi and noto tate are employed from the knee, and the swordsman ends in seiza.

KATA USHIRO (REAR FORM)

From seiza, prepare to utilize nuki-dashi tate, after glancing over the left shoulder to the rear (the back of the right hand should be already seated on the tsuka at the time of the glance) (14.24, 14.25). As the saya is withdrawn from the blade, rise to the right knee (14.26). Stand and parry the blade overhead, spinning counterclockwise by sliding the left foot back, 180

14.26

14.27

14.28

14.29

degrees to the rear (14.27). Grip the bottom of the tsuka with the left hand (14.28), and execute shomen-uchi, while dropping to the left knee (14.29). Execute chiburi and noto tate from the knee, and then sit back into seiza. Rotate 180 degrees clockwise, back to the original direction, spinning on the knees and holding the sword securely with both hands.

KATA MAE, USHIRO CHOKUZEN (FRONT, REAR CENTER-LEVEL THRUST FORM)

From seiza, employ nuki-dashi tomoe to the front (14.30), and parry the blade into shomen-uchi (in the same posture) (14.31, 14.32). While down on the left knee, turn 90 degrees to the left, and rotate the kissaki 180 degrees to the rear, so that the blade is perpendicular to the front (14.33, 14.34). With the fingers together, pointing toward the front, place your left hand onto the mune, and execute mae-tsuki

14.30

14.31

14.32

14.33

14.34

14.35

14.36

14.37

14.38

14.39

(similar to the manner in which a pool cue is used) toward the original, rear direction, with a forward (14.35) and back (14.36) sliding motion. Be certain to look in the direction of the thrust. Finish by standing, then turning 90 degrees on the right foot to the left (14.37), in the direction of the mae-tsuki, and parrying the blade for a shomen-uchi, shifting the left foot back and settling onto the left knee (14.38). Perform chiburi and noto tate from the knee. After sitting into seiza, spin clockwise on the knees, returning to the original, frontal position.

KATA HIDARI, MAE NUKI-UCHI (LEFT, FRONT JUMP-CUT FORM)

From seiza, glance quickly to the left (14.39), then to the front, and prepare to perform nuki-dashi tate (14.40). The draw is executed by shifting off the right knee onto the left knee, and turning 90 degrees to the left, completing the draw (14.41) and following

14.40

14.41

14.42

14.43

14.44

14.45

14.46

14.47

14.48

14.49

with a shomen-uchi (14.42). On the left knee, turn 90 degrees to the original frontal direction (right), and position the left hand on the mune (14.43, 14.44) to execute tomoe sasse-uchi to the front (14.45). Next, stand (14.46), and slide the left foot forward into hidari zenkutsu-dachi, simultaneously turning the ha downward, blade at the hip (14.47). Perform mae-tsuki with the right hand on the tsuka (using the "pool cue" method), to the front (14.48, 14.49). Last, with the right hand, parry the blade counterclockwise across the

14.50

14.51

14.52

14.53

14.54

front and over the head, and then grasp the bottom of the tsuka with the left hand, while performing nuki-uchi (jump-cut) (14.50). The feet land in opposite positions, with the left leg shifting to the rear, onto the knee, and the right foot to the front (14.51). Perform chiburi and noto tate on the knee. Sit in seiza.

KATA JODEN-UKE (UPPER-LEVEL BLOCK FORM)

From seiza, execute nuki-dashi tate by turning the ha in the left direction, and bringing the sheathed sword diagonally up across the front of the body, so that the tsuba is approximately at chin level at the right side of the head (14.52). Unsheathe the sword while rising off the right knee (14.53), ending in joden-uke (upper-level block) position (14.54). Parry the blade overhead (14.55), and perform a two-handed kubi-uchi in place (14.56). Perform chiburi by letting go of the tsuka with the right hand, and striking it close to the tsuba with the bottom of the fist (14.57, 14.58). This action would knock some of the blood off

14.55

14.56

14.57

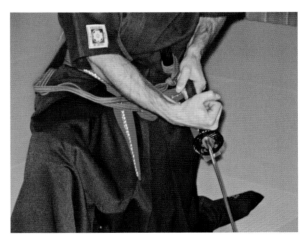

14.58

the blade in a battle situation. With the right hand, again grab the tsuka, utilizing a reverse grip (14.59, 14.60), and then release it with the left hand. Turn over the tsuka with a quick, snapping motion (rotating the palm upward), bringing the kissaki down, then upward, at the left side of the body. Meet the mune with the koiguchi (14.61) for noto tate, utilizing this reverse grip, while still on the left knee. Sit in seiza.

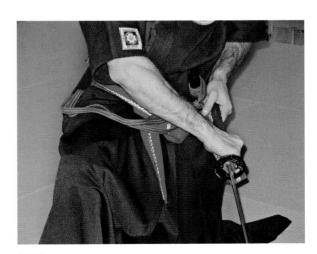

14.59

14.60

14.61

KATA USHIRO, MAE (REAR, FRONT FORM)

From seiza, execute nuki-dashi ushiro while rising off the right knee, and thrust the sword to the rear, at the right side of the body (14.62). (The mune should be positioned flat against the bottom of the forearm prior to the thrust. This will set the blade parallel to the ground when the thrust has been completed.) In place, rotate the ha from the downward direction toward the right, and execute a tomoe-uchi horizontally across the front of the body, without changing the grip on the tsuka (14.63). Loosen the grip with the right hand (14.64), and bring the end of the tsuka up to the left side of the head, while turning the ha upward with the left hand. Slide the right hand forward, so that the mune drops onto the palm. Here the fingers are close together, pointed forward, and the kissaki is pointed to the front, extending beyond the nose

14.62

14.63

14.64

14.65

14.66

14.67

(14.65). Thrust the blade straight ahead from this position (using the "pool cue" method) (14.66, 14.67), and then finish by sliding the right hand, with the palm upward, back up the mune, under the tsuba (14.68), and onto the bottom side of the tsuka. Grab the tsuka (14.69), and perform gyaku kubi-uchi by parrying overhead (14.70, 14.71). Perform chiburi and noto tate from the knee. Return to seiza.

14.68

14.69

14.70

14.71

14.72

14.73

KATA OROSHI (MOUNTAIN WIND FORM)

From seiza, bring the sheathed blade slightly forward from the iai obi, while positioning the back of the right hand on top of the tsuka, as if about to draw (14.72). Retract the sword back into the iai obi, while turning over the right hand and grabbing the tsuka. Follow by quickly rising off the right knee (14.73), and thrusting the sheathed blade forward (14.74) and back, executing kashira-uchi (pommel strike). Stand (14.75) and execute nuki-dashi tate into joden-uke, as if executing the draw-

14.74

14.75

14.76

14.77

ing method employed in kata joden-uke, only now from a standing position (14.76). After the blade has been unsheathed, spin counterclockwise on the back, left foot. Slide the right foot 180 degrees to the left, while parrying the blade overhead with the right hand, to execute a one-handed, yokumen-uchi (horizontal neck-cut) to the rear (14.77, 14.78, 14.79). Continue the counterclockwise turn, pivoting on the left foot, and slide the right foot to the original frontal direction, keeping the blade at neck level, with the arm extended and rotating the sword like a helicopter propeller (14.80). After the kissaki has cleared the front of the body, with the ha still angled toward the left, parry the blade overhead (14.81), grab the tsuka with the left hand (14.82, 14.83), and drop onto the left knee, executing shomen-uchi (14.84). Perform chiburi and noto tate from the knee. Return to seiza.

14.78

14.79

14.80

14.81

14.82

14.83

14.84

Conclusion

I realize that it is very unlikely that a contemporary practitioner would need to use a samurai sword to defend honor, country, or self. Many beginners as well as advanced martial artists have asked me why I perceive samurai sword training as an integral element of Japanese and Okinawan martial arts study. My response is based on the fact that samurai sword techniques were the template for almost all of the original combat martial arts that were developed by the samurai—the samurai sword was their primary weapon, and ken-jutsu and iai-jutsu were their primary arts. Studying the techniques of the samurai sword provides a foundation for understanding the other martial arts of the samurai. Practicing the techniques of the samurai sword helps to improve overall martial arts technique, with or without the sword. At the same time, training in this effective and eloquent weapon keeps an old art from extinction.

Now that you have come to more fully comprehend the essence of iai-jutsu and ken-jutsu, you may be contemplating beginning your own training. Ideally, if you have access to a martial arts dojo or to classes taught at another facility, under the direction of a *certified* instructor in iai-jutsu and/or ken-jutsu, I'd recommend that you observe a class to see if it is right for you. Try searching the Internet, or look in a local telephone book to ascertain the availability of classes in your area.

If, after reading this book, you find yourself inspired to become a swordsperson, but cannot locate a place where training of this type is available, you can go about your sword training by yourself. Follow this book in the order in which I have presented the techniques, and refer to the DVD, an invaluable tool for solo practice.

Glossary

Age sasse-uchi   Supported, upward vertical cut

Age-uchi   Diagonal rising cut

Ashi-uchi   Leg cut

Bogyo-waza   Defense techniques

Boshi   The tempered part of the blade, located just above the fukura

Bushi   Warrior

Chiburi   Deblood

Chiburi ichi-waza   Deblooding technique #1

Chiburi ni-waza   Deblooding technique #2

Choji oil   Type of oil used for the samurai sword

Chokuto   Japanese sword with a straight blade, modeled after the Chinese type

Chuburi seiza   Seated deblood

Chuden kumai   Center-level guard

Chuden-uke   Mid-level block

Daimyo   Lord, or a samurai's master

Daisho   A pair of swords, made up of the shoto and daito

Daito   Long samurai sword

Dojo   Training hall

Enbusen   The beginning and ending position in a kata

Fuchi-gane   The cover protecting the open end of the tsuka

Fukasa-Ryu   Profound Martial Arts Style

Fukura   The sharpened area at the end of the blade below the kissaki

Gedan kumai   Lower-level guard

Gedan-uke   Lower-level block

Gyaku age-uchi   Reverse diagonal rising cut

Gyaku joden-uke   Reverse upper-level block

Gyaku kubi-uchi   Diagonal reverse neck cut

Gyaku-no kumai   Reverse guard

Gyaku tomoe-uchi   Reverse horizontal stomach cut

Gyaku yokumen-uchi   Reverse side of head cut (reverse horizontal cut to neck)

Ha   The cutting edge or sharpened part of the blade

Habaki   The collar on the samurai sword located just below the ha-machi and mune-machi

Hai   Yes

Hajame   Begin (a command)

Hakama   Uniform skirt

Ha-machi   The location marking the beginning of the Ha just beyond the tang

Hamon   Temper line on the blade

Han-sankyo   Kneeling position with one knee touching the ground

Hara   Area of the body located around the lower abdominal cavity

Hasso-no kumai   Vertical guard

Heisoku-dachi   Ready stance

Hi   Blood groove

Hidari   Left

Hidari rei-nochi dachi   Left fencer's stance

Hidari zenkutsu-dachi   Left locked-leg stance

Hitoe   The upper part of the tang of the sword

Hiza-mazuku   Down to the knee position (a command)

Iai-jutsu   The art of drawing the samurai sword most expeditiously

Iai-jutsu ka   Iai-jutsu practitioner

Iai obi   Sword belt

Iaito   Unsharpened, metal practice sword used for kata

Jien   Chinese pronunciation of the word for "sword"

Jigane   The area between the hamon and the shinogi

Joden-kumai   Upper-level guard

Joden-uke   Upper-level block

Ka   Practitioner

Kashira   The cap protecting the end of the tsuka

Kashira-uchi   Pommel strike

Kata   A form or contrived sequence of movements

Katana   Revised type of tachi, with shortened blade length

Katana-ni-rei   Bow to honor the katana (a command)

Kaze   Wind

Keba-dachi   Horse stance (legs wide apart with knees bent deeply)

Keikogi   Woven jacket for samurai sword practice

Ken Japanese pronunciation of the word for "sword"

Ken-jutsu The art of fencing with the unsheathed samurai sword

Ken-jutsu ka Ken-jutsu practitioner

Kio-tsuke Attention! (a command)

Kiru Cut, slice

Kissaki The upper portion of the end of the blade, ending at the blade tip

Kobu-jutsu The samurai fighting arts

Koiguchi The mouth of the scabbard (saya)

Kojiri The cap closing the back of the scabbard

Ko-shinogi Extension of the shinogi beyond the yokote

Kubi-uchi Diagonal neck-cut

Kumai-waza Guard positions

Kurigata The knob on the scabbard holding the rope (sageo)

Mae aruku ni Two steps forward (a command)

Mae-tsuki Front thrust

Mae ukemi Front fall

Mae zempo kaiten Front rotary rolls

Mei The swordsmith's inscription on the tang

Mekugi Small bamboo piece holding the hilt to the tang

Mekugi-ana Peg-hole in the tang

Mekuginuki Small brass hammer

Menuki Grip-enhancing ornaments on the tsuka

Migi Right

Migi rei-nochi dachi Right fencer's stance

Migi zenkutsu-dachi Right locked-leg stance

Mitsukado The junction of the shinogi, ko-shinogi, and yokote

Monouchi The "maximum strike" area of the blade, comprising the last quarter of the ha

Mune Top of the blunted portion of the blade

Mune-machi The location marking the beginning of the mune, just beyond the tang

Mune sasse-uchi Supported chest-level, horizontal cut

Mushin "No-mindedness"

Musubi-dachi Posture with heels together and feet directed at opposite, oblique angles

Nakago The lower part of the tang of the sword

Nakago-jiri The end of the tang

Naname-no-katana Samurai sword in the "port of arms" position (a command)

Nito-waza Double-sword techniques

Noto Sheathing

Noto tate Vertical sheathing

Noto tomoe Horizontal stomach sheathing

Nuki-dashi Draw

Nuki-dashi age Rising oblique draw

Nuki-dashi seiza Seated draw

Nuki-dashi tate Vertical draw

Nuki-dashi tomoe Horizontal stomach draw

Nuki-dashi ushiro Rear draw

Nuki-uchi Jump-cut

Obi Sash or belt

Oroshi Mountain wind

Rank obi The belt that represents your rank

Rei Bow

Rei-nochi dachi Fencer's stance

Ryu School of thought, style

Sageo Rope hung from the sword's scabbard

Sageo musubi Tie the sageo (a command)

Saho Formal etiquette

Samei Ray skin (on the tsuka)

Samurai A retainer who acted in the interests of his daimyo (lord) and the country of Japan

Sasse-uchi Supported cut

Saya Scabbard

Seiza A seated position with feet behind the buttocks

Sensei ni taishite no rei Bow with honor to the teacher (a command)

Sempai The most senior student

Seppa Washers that surround the hand guard of the sword

Seppuku Ritual suicide

Shikaze Four winds

Shikko-waza   Techniques for moving on the knees

Shinogi   The longitudinal ridge located above the jigane

Shinogi-ji   The area located between the shinogi and mune

Shizentai-dachi   Natural posture

Shogunate   A military style of leadership

Shomen   "Head" of the dojo where the headmaster stands at "bow-in"

Shomen-uchi   Vertical head cut

Shoto   Smaller, auxiliary sword

Suburi   Cutting

Suburito   Heavy wooden sword used in training

Tachi   A samurai sword model, at least four feet long, worn suspended from the hip, with its cutting edge downward

Taito   Seat the sword (a command)

Taitsukiryu-o-hakama   You may get dressed (a command)

Tang (an English word)   The unsharpened portion of the blade that is under the hilt of the sword

Tanto   Knife

Tatame   Matted area of practice hall

Tate-no-katana   Bring the sword to the vertical position (a command)

Tatsu   Stand up (a command)

Te-moto   Hand positioning

Tomoe-uchi   Horizontal stomach cut

Tsuba   Hand guard

Tsuba-uke   Hand guard block

Tsugi-ashi   Following-foot movements

Tsuka   Hilt

Tsuka-ito   Cord wrapped around the tsuka

Uchiko   Powder hammer

Ukemi-waza   Falling techniques

Uke-waza   Blocking techniques

Ushiro aruku ni   Back two steps (a command)

Ushiro-tsuki   Rear thrust

Uwagi   Uniform jacket

Waka-no kumai   Side guard

Wakizashi   Short samurai sword

Washi   Large cloth

Waza   Techniques

Yakiba   Tempered area of the blade

Yin and yang   Offensive and defensive principles of attack

Yokote   The latitudinal line that separates the ha from the fukura

Yoko ukemi   Side fall

Yokumen-uchi   Side of head cut (horizontal cut to neck)

Acknowledgments

I want to acknowledge all the people who helped bring this text to completion. First and foremost, I want to thank my mother, Sandy Nemeroff, for playing a most integral role in editing the entire manuscript, including text and pictures. Without her, this work would have not appeared so eloquent in every facet.

I also want to thank both of my parents for enrolling me in the martial arts as a young boy. Their persistence and constant encouragement throughout my life continue to give me the confidence to pursue my dreams.

And my wife, Tsen-Ting, who understands and appreciates the commitment that I have to the martial arts, re-ignited my interest in writing this book and regularly motivated me in this endeavor until its conclusion.

I want to honor my teacher, Rod Sacharnoski, Soke, who continues to inspire me through his philosophy and mastery of martial arts technique. It is his generosity, trust, and patience that have sculpted me into the martial artist that I am today. I am honored that he would write such a foreword for this book.

Next, I thank my student Greg Zenon, Kyoshi, the "Fukasa-Kai Photographer" who photographed all the fabulous pictures in this text, for forgoing the opportunity to demonstrate your proficient iai/ken-jutsu technique, in order to share your masterful skills as a photographer.

To David George, Sensei, for allowing me to utilize his beautiful dojo, Lehigh Fukasa-Kai, which captures the essence of an ideal dojo setting.

And my thanks to all my devoted students who contributed in some way through the pictures of this text: D. Nemeroff, Shihan; G. Zenon, Kyoshi; A. Cabrera, Kyoshi; N. Gordon, Sensei; D. DerSarkisian, Sensei; D. George, Sensei; and L. Hernandez. Thank you all for donating your time, energy, and positive attitudes during that long and enduring day of pictures that extended into the early hours of the next morning. I am honored to have such fine students, who put their hearts, souls, and skills into this aspect of the publication.

Author's Biography

A teacher of the Okinawan and Japanese martial arts, Cary Nemeroff has merged his interests in education, persons with disabilities, and the Asian combat arts into a full-time career. He has earned a B.A. in philosophy from New York University as well as an M.A. in education from Teachers College, Columbia University. He also has studied and is proficient in sign language. His martial arts training began as a young boy in 1977, under the auspices of Juko-Kai International, a martial arts organization accredited in both Okinawa and the mainland of Japan. His passion and skills as a martial artist grew in adolescence, and he ultimately became the personal student of Dr. Rod Sacharnoski, president of Juko-Kai International. This relationship continues today. Cary has earned ninth-degree black belts in a variety of Okinawan and Japanese samurai martial arts, including iai-jutsu and ken-jutsu, the subject of this book. And he recently earned tenth dan recognition in Fukasa-Ryu *bujutsu* that includes iai-jutsu and ken-jutsu as well.

Cary is founder and president of Fukasa-Ryu Bujutsu Kai, a martial arts organization that is a member of the International Okinawan Martial Arts Union and is accredited and sponsored by the Zen Kokusai Soke Budo/Bugei Renmei.

At present, Cary conducts an extensive program of group classes for adults and children, including specialized classes for children with physical and cognitive challenges such as autism, at the Jewish Community Center in Manhattan, a state-of-the-art fitness and cultural facility located on New York's Upper West Side. Among the martial arts he teaches are the samurai sword (iai-jutsu and ken-jutsu), *aiki-jujutsu* (a Japanese, bare-handed method of self-defense used by the samurai to disarm an armed opponent), karate, and *toide* (Okinawan throwing and grappling). At other venues, he also provides individual instruction and training, and conducts clinics for schools affiliated with his own organization.

He can be reached through the Fukasa Kai website, www.fukasakai.com.

About the DVD

Mastering the Samurai Sword is sold with an informational DVD, which should be affixed to the facing page. It features demonstrations of all of the techniques in this book performed by its author, Cary Nemeroff. A useful resource for both beginners and experienced swordspeople, it will help you perfect your practice by showing you in real time how each move should be executed.

On this DVD, you will learn about:

Preparing to practice
Putting on the hakama
Tying the rank obi
Preparing the sword

Ken-jutsu
Cuts
- Shomen-uchi
- Kubi-uchi
- Tomoe-uchi
- Nuki-uchi
- Age-uchi
- Yokumen-uchi
- Mae-tsuki
- Sasse-uchi
- Ushiro-tsuki

Blocking & Evasive Techniques
- Joden-uke
- Tsuba-uke
- Chuden-uke
- Gedan-uke

Falling & Knee-Walking Techniques
- Mae ukemi
- Yoko ukemi
- Mae zempo kaiten
- Shikko-waza

Iai-jutsu
Drawing the sword
- Nuki-dashi age
- Nuki-dashi tate
- Nuki-dashi tomoe
- Nuki-dashi ushiro
- Nuki-dashi seiza

Deblooding
- Chiburi ichi-waza
- Chiburi ni-waza
- Chiburi seiza

Sheathing the sword
- Noto tomoe
- Noto tate
- Noto seiza

Standing Forms
- Kata mae
- Kata migi
- Kata hidari
- Kata ushiro
- Kata kaze kiru
- Kata ushiro nuki-uchi
- Kata migi, hidari, mae
- Kata shikaze

Kneeling Forms
- Kata mae
- Kata migi
- Kata hidari, mae
- Kata ushiro
- Kata mae, ushiro chokuzen
- Kata hidari, mae nuki-uchi
- Kata joden-uke
- Kata ushiro, mae
- Kata oroshi

Preparing the Sword for Storage